GRASSROOTS TYRANNY

The Limits of Federalism

CLINT BOLICK

CATO
INSTITUTE
Washington D.C.

Library of Congress Cataloging-in-Publication Data

Bolick, Clint.
    Grassroots tyranny : the limits of federalism / Clint Bolick.
        p.   cm.
    Includes bibliographical references and index.
    ISBN 1-882577-01-9 (hardback) : $21.95.—ISBN 1-882577-00-0
(pbk.) : $12.95
    1. Civil rights—United States.   2. Federal government—United
States.   3. State governments—United States.   4. Local
government—United States.   I. Title.
JC599.U5B5575   1993   93-3957
323.4′9′0973—dc20   CIP

Printed in the United States of America.

CATO INSTITUTE
1000 Massachusetts Ave., N.W.
Washington, D.C. 20001

GRASSROOTS TYRANNY

For my son,
Todd Garrison Bolick,
a spirited individualist

Contents

Acknowledgments

This book is a hybrid, combining a philosophical and historical dissertation on federalism with real-world, journalistic-style accounts of grassroots tyranny. As a result, the research requirements were daunting, particularly for someone whose primary vocation is not writing but litigation.

I could not have produced this book without tremendous assistance and inspiration from Mary Chlopecki. Had she not agreed at a Baltimore Orioles game in the summer of 1988 to assist in the project, it never would have come to fruition. In addition to gathering data on grassroots tyranny from sources far and wide, Mary drafted significant portions of chapters 6 (property rights) and 7 (freedom of speech) and contributed to much of the rest. The book is enriched tremendously by her editing prowess, insights, and humor.

The book's other indispensable partner is the Cato Institute, and I am indebted especially to Ed Crane, David Boaz, and Roger Pilon. As anyone who knows them will agree, they are first-rate professionals and philosophical taskmasters, and I delight in my every collaboration with them. In addition to sponsoring, editing, publishing, and marketing this book, the Cato Institute has stood behind me throughout my career as a public interest lawyer, and I am enormously grateful for its support.

Numerous organizations and individuals contributed examples of grassroots tyranny, many of which appear in these chapters. Special thanks to Ira Glasser and the American Civil Liberties Union (ACLU); Arthur Eisenberg and the New York Civil Liberties Union; the ACLU of Northern California; the ACLU Foundation of Southern California; Timothy Bittle and the Pacific Legal Foundation; Brian Summers, Bettina Greaves, and the Foundation for Economic Education; Sam Kazman and the Competitive Enterprise Institute; Virginia Postrel and the Reason Foundation; David Keating and the National Taxpayers Union; Joe Bast and the Heartland Institute;

Mark Bredemeier and Landmark Legal Foundation; Henry Butler, George Mason University School of Law; Jane Shaw and the Political Economy Research Center; Jonathan Emord of the Cato Institute; Dave Kehler and the Public Affairs Research Institute of New Jersey; Dan Lavey and Oregonians in Action; James Taranto; and Mary Lynn (Rasmussen) Chess, the "Okie Girl." I hope I haven't forgotten anyone! Additional technical support was supplied by Julie Chlopecki, who painstakingly cite-checked the manuscript.

Some of the individuals whose encounters with grassroots tyranny are described in this book are or were clients of mine: Taalibdin Abdul Uqdah and Pamela Ferrell, Alfredo Santos, Ego Brown, Stuart Marsh, and Stanley Dea. These people are heroes in the tradition of Rosa Parks, who refused to sit in the back of the bus. Their courage inspires me ceaselessly.

Sometimes the ordeals they faced have happy endings. As this book was going to press, Uqdah and Ferrell's 10-year struggle to save their hairbraiding business (see chapter 9) finally succeeded: on December 15, 1992, the District of Columbia city council, faced with litigation by the Institute for Justice and extensive media attention, voted to deregulate the cosmetology profession. Those two entrepreneurs' triumph against grassroots tyranny marks an important milestone in the quest to restore economic liberty in America.

Last but not least, I thank my colleagues at the Institute for Justice, especially Chip Mellor and Scott Bullock, as well as our directors and supporters, not only for their enthusiasm for this book, but for providing the most congenial and stimulating base from which to wage the battle for liberty in the courts.

If anything, this book illustrates the enormity of the task ahead. Ordinarily, at this point I'd quote something inspirational from my hero, Tom Paine. Instead I'll quote the modern sage Yogi Berra, who aptly stated, "It ain't over 'til it's over." To my aforementioned friends, I say, The road ahead may prove treacherous, but there's no one I'd rather travel it with than you.

Introduction

For most people, federalism is an abstraction, one of those murky concepts that crops up in high school civics or college political science classes. At best, federalism is vaguely understood as a notion that was important during the American founding era, having something to do with a preference for local over national government because of its proximity to the people. Given the modern growth and power of national government, most people would likely consider federalism a quaint anachronism.

That is true even though federalism issues are at the core of many contemporary legal battles that touch upon matters of great importance to individuals, ranging from abortion to taxation, economic regulation, freedom of speech, and private-property rights. Unfortunately, those charged with the responsibility of applying the principles of federalism in such cases seem not to understand them any better than the typical person on the street. This confusion about federalism and its proper role in our constitutional system has produced effects that are extremely deleterious to individual liberty. The most serious of those effects is the phenomenon of grassroots tyranny, the abuse of individual rights by local governments.

I first encountered grassroots tyranny long before I knew anything about federalism. Although I did not fully appreciate the significance of this experience at the time, it left a vivid impression on me.

This initial encounter occurred when I was growing up in the suburban city of Linden, New Jersey. By ninth grade, I had developed a lively interest in politics and decided to involve myself at the local level. I discovered that Linden's politics were completely dominated by the city's autocratic mayor, John T. Gregorio. Indulging a tendency that has recurred fairly constantly since then, I aligned myself with the underdog—in this instance, a retired insurance executive named Joe Locascio, Mayor Gregorio's nemesis and

1

the only Republican on the 11-member city council. Locascio took me under his wing, teaching me that principle is more important than expediency, and delighting me with such witticisms as "When you vote for the elephant or the donkey, that's what you get," and (in an allusion to the famous "silent majority" slogan of the Nixon era) "The majority is not silent, the government is deaf!"

Generally, Joe Locascio was to the mayor little more than a nuisance. But over time, his persistence paid off. Forcing a ballot initiative, he took away the mayor's most prized possession—his power to appoint the board of education and thereby to control an enormous reservoir of patronage and influence. The advent of an elected school board was Joe Locascio's greatest triumph and John Gregorio's most humiliating defeat.

But Locascio's success was short-lived. Following the election of a second Republican to the city council, Locascio was subjected to a vicious smear campaign that compelled him to resign his office in 1974. Since then, Linden has experienced virtually unchallenged one-party rule.

I revisited this experience in the context of a college thesis[1] in which I analyzed the Linden situation within a political science framework. What Mayor Gregorio was operating was a classic political machine. Far from disappearing with the death of the infamous Chicago mayor Richard J. Daley, these machines, I discovered, were moving to the suburbs. A bit more subtle and sophisticated than the notorious political machines of days past, the Gregorio machine was no less corrupt or oppressive. The machine severely punished its adversaries and lavishly rewarded its supporters, constantly wielding the apparatus of local government to perpetuate its own existence and expand its power. Gregorio operated the city as his personal fiefdom.

Not all the machine's activities were within the boundaries of the law, and eventually Mayor Gregorio was convicted on criminal charges and stripped of his elected offices. But in early 1990, as one of his final official acts, Governor Thomas Kean pardoned

---

[1] Clint Bolick, " 'Hooray for Me, to Hell with You': The Contemporary Suburban Political Machine," honors thesis, Drew University, 1979.

Gregorio, who thereupon promptly sought and regained his old position as mayor.[2]

No sooner did Gregorio return to office than he resumed his old tricks. Shortly after his inauguration, he demanded that the police chief—a civil servant who had not supported Gregorio's election—assign two police officers to serve as his personal chauffeurs. The police chief refused, whereupon Gregorio suspended him. The chief appealed, and Gregorio appointed himself as hearing officer to preside over and rule upon the appeal. Thus Gregorio the defendant was also Gregorio the judge—a perfect combination by which to perpetuate a regime of tyranny.[3]

This apparently continuing episode of grassroots tyranny in my hometown had a significant impact on me, for it dispelled any illusion I might have had of local governments as models of Jeffersonian democracy. Yet I might have chalked up the Linden experience as an aberration had I not elected to pursue my legal studies in Davis, California, where I encountered grassroots tyranny of a different sort.

The Davis city government was controlled during the early 1980s by the Campaign for Economic Democracy (CED), whose strategy was to use the coercive power of government to redistribute wealth in a way the organization deemed equitable.[4] CED focused not on government at the national or state level (although California governor Jerry Brown actively promoted CED's efforts, particularly through judicial appointments), but on local government. Led by Tom Hayden and bankrolled by Jane Fonda, CED sponsored candidates for local nonpartisan offices and secured appointments to municipal planning and zoning boards. CED members won control of several California cities, including Davis, Berkeley, and Santa Monica.

CED's primary goal was to diminish private-property rights and to redistribute wealth to those who did not own property. The group pushed stringent rent-control, antigrowth, and planning

---

[2]Ironically, Kean is now president of my alma mater, Drew University, under whose auspices I had conducted my study chronicling the sordid record of Mayor Gregorio.

[3]See Nicolas Veronis, "Linden Mayor to Head Disciplinary Hearing for Police Chief He Suspended," (Newark, N.J.) *Star-Ledger*, January 13, 1991, sec. 1, p. 29.

[4]See Justin Raimondo, "Inside the CED," *Reason* (February 1982), p. 17.

laws. No exercise of property rights was too trivial to escape the scrutiny of the city's planning bureaucrats. Property owners had to endure countless hearings and lectures about social responsibility if they were to have the slightest chance of developing their property, and even then were subject to stringent controls. They were told by city planners what colors they had to paint their houses, which direction the houses had to face, how many windows the houses could have, and even how much money they lawfully could make if they sold their houses.

These supposedly benign restrictions produced perverse consequences. In Davis, growth controls and regulatory burdens caused the cost of housing to skyrocket. Meanwhile, the combination of rent control and strict limits on development produced a chronic shortage of rental housing for college students. CED attributed these consequences not to overzealous local government but to greedy speculators.

CED also fostered a repressive political environment. Because the organization's members viewed themselves as part of a moral crusade, they attempted persistently to suppress opposition and to impugn the motives of their adversaries. In Davis, the city council passed a law restricting campaign contributions to $35, thus limiting the ability of the victims of CED's tyranny to effectively challenge it through the political process. Though professedly liberal, CED had little use for the First Amendment once its members controlled the reins of government.

CED knew what it was doing. The organization's agenda, as one observer summarized it, was based on the premise that "the political power of city government can be used to control and reallocate wealth at the local level."[5] And in city after city, CED proved this theory correct. Ironically, just as Ronald Reagan was winning election as president and promising a reduction of government control over many aspects of people's lives, CED was launching a counterrevolution at the grassroots level. As former solicitor general Charles Fried has remarked, "At a time when the federal

---

[5]Paul Ciotti, "Socialism . . . On the Street Where You Live," *Reason* (April 1981), p. 26.

government was committed to loosening the regulations that hampered economic efficiency, political entrepreneurs [were] let loose at the local level, at the expense of the public and of consumers."[6]

The Davis experience demonstrated again to me how far we have traveled from the days of town meeting democracy. For local government today consists not so much of elected officials as of appointed bureaucrats with enormous powers and little accountability to the public. Indeed, in today's society a zoning commissioner or a tax assessor can have far greater impact on personal liberties than the president of the United States. Yet typical Americans, including me, probably cannot name a single one of these powerful people in their own communities.

Since graduating from law school, I have spent much of my time prosecuting lawsuits against local governments for various constitutional violations, particularly in the areas of racial discrimination and economic liberty. At the same time, I have worked with municipal governments in cases where in their efforts to safeguard individual liberties they were challenged in court. But the sum of my experiences suggests that local governments today too often play the role of violators rather than protectors of basic individual rights. As Sam Staley concluded in a 1992 study for the Cato Institute, "Local governments, like all governments, act as Leviathan, exploiting constituents to further enhance their own power and authority."[7]

That was not supposed to happen. The primary purpose of the Framers of the American republic in embracing federalism as the organizational system of government was to safeguard individual liberty. As Lino Graglia defines it, "Federalism is the attempt to minimize the loss of liberty [that occurs when individuals form governments] by requiring that decision-making authority be removed from the individual as little far as possible."[8] This doctrinal preference for the most decentralized possible government was one

[6]Charles Fried, *Order and Law* (New York: Simon & Schuster, 1991), p. 187.

[7]Sam Staley, "Bigger Is Not Better: The Virtues of Decentralized Local Government," *Cato Policy Analysis* no. 166 (January 21, 1992), p. 35.

[8]Lino A. Graglia, "Restoring the Federalist System: How to Return Control of Local Affairs to Local Authority," unpublished manuscript prepared for the Advisory Commission on Intergovernmental Relations, p. 1.

of the principal constitutional mechanisms designed to secure a free society.

The Framers recognized, however, that unchecked government power at any level is inherently destructive of individual liberty. This concern was echoed by Alexis de Tocqueville, who warned of the dangers of too-powerful local government a century and a half ago in *Democracy in America*. "When tyranny is established in the bosom of a small state," he observed, "it is more galling than elsewhere, because, acting in a narrower circle, everything in that circle is affected by it." Such tyranny is accomplished, de Tocqueville explained, by the state's "exasperating interference in a multitude of minute details," going beyond the "political world, to which it properly belongs, to meddle with arrangements of private life. Tastes as well as actions are to be regulated."[9] Ultimately, that amounts to the pervasive control of individual affairs that characterizes local government today. De Tocqueville predicted that America's federal system would prevent such abuses, but clearly it has not.

The reasons for and consequences of that failure are the subject of this book. In the following pages, I argue that two major developments have thwarted federalism's capacity to fulfill its central role in promoting a free society. The first is demographic. As Thomas J. Anton has observed, "Federalism has helped to produce the most 'governed' state in the world: At last count, more than 82,000 separate units of government" existed in the United States.[10] That does not include state and local regulatory boards, which exercise some of the most sweeping powers of government.

The growth of the local leviathan is explosive: in the 1970s alone, 2,000 new local government units were created.[11] State and local governments comprise 500,000 elected officials and 13 million appointed officials, compared with 2 million civilian employees at the federal level.[12] State bureaucracies grew by 19 percent during

[9]Alexis de Tocqueville, "Advantages of the Federal System in General, and Its Special Utility in America," reprinted in *Taking the Constitution Seriously*, ed. Gary L. McDowell (Dubuque, Iowa: Kendall/Hunt Publishing Co., 1981), p. 189.

[10]Thomas J. Anton, *American Federalism and Public Policy* (New York: Random House, 1989), p. 4.

[11]Ibid., p. 6.

[12]Ibid., p. 4.

the 1980s, more than twice as fast as the national population[13]; spending by the states doubled during the same period, from $258 billion in 1980 to $525 billion in 1989.[14]

What that means is that the Framers' image of local government as responsive to the citizenry has long since grown obsolete. If the original model of direct participatory democracy operates at all today, its existence is limited to a handful of communities that somehow cling to New England–style town meetings. But such instances are rare. Instead, many of the most powerful mechanisms of local government today are hidden from view, and are both antidemocratic and destructive of individual rights.

The second development leading to the demise of federalism is the abandonment of the traditional principles of federalism. Almost no one today defends the original purpose of federalism as promoting individual liberty. Rather, two general positions on federalism have emerged. On one side, most liberals generally favor national power over state or local authority. But they also favor expansive local government powers when they are exercised to achieve social or economic justice, even if that means sweeping restrictions on individual autonomy. On the other side, many conservatives also have lost sight of the original principles of federalism, favoring states' rights as an end in itself, rather than as a means to the greater end of protecting individual liberty. In this conservative construct, federalism operates as a shield for abuses of rights by local governments instead of as a protection for those rights, as it originally was intended to provide.

The leading proponent of states' rights federalism is Robert Bork. In *The Tempting of America*, Bork constructed a constitutional rationale for broad local government sovereignty with little concern for individual rights.[15] He has dismissed those who see the world differently for their "endless exploration of abstract philosophical principles."[16]

[13]Andrew Bates, "Blame Game," *The New Republic*, November 4, 1991, p. 11.

[14]Virginia I. Postrel, "The States Are Becoming the New 'Big Government,' " *Washington Post*, July 14, 1991, p. C3.

[15]See generally Robert H. Bork, *The Tempting of America* (New York: Free Press, 1990).

[16]Robert H. Bork, *Tradition and Morality in Constitutional Law* (Washington: American Enterprise Institute for Public Policy Research, 1984), p. 9.

With all due respect to Bork, I believe that an inquiry into the principles that animated the Framers' commitment to federalism is critical to understanding and correcting what has gone wrong. Such an inquiry can have important real-world consequences. As Cass Sunstein has noted, "State governments are peculiarly susceptible to capture by groups bent on distributing wealth or opportunities in their own favor."[17] Theories involving federalism, Sunstein concludes, may therefore provide a framework to check abuses of government power. If the concept of federalism can be revitalized as a meaningful safeguard of basic liberties, it would mark a significant milestone in our centuries-old quest to ensure a free society.

In this book, I attempt to describe and illustrate the nature and ramifications of this quandary. I begin by exploring the origins and evolution of American federalism, focusing on its metamorphosis from a liberty-enhancing system into one that has sanctioned myriad violations of liberty by local government. I then present examples of grassroots tyranny that are in whole or part attributable to this mutated concept of federalism. I conclude with a framework for revitalizing federalism to fulfill the Framers' objective of maximizing individual liberty, a framework characterized by a robust balance of powers between federal and local governments and a preference for whichever promotes liberty.

The following discussion of specific instances of grassroots tyranny is wide-ranging, covering various areas in which individual autonomy is supplanted by government control. I do not suggest that every law regulating individual action is improper. Likewise, I do not at all intend to denigrate the institution of local government or the thousands of well-meaning public servants who serve at the state or local level. The machinery of local government certainly can be, and often is, used for the public good. But the existence of this awesome power, shielded to a large extent from public scrutiny, too often provides an irresistible temptation to those who would use it for evil purposes.

The examples of grassroots tyranny set forth in this book illustrate the pervasiveness of local government in regulating almost every aspect of personal behavior. In this respect, these instances barely

---

[17]Cass R. Sunstein, "Naked Preferences and the Constitution," *Columbia Law Review* 84 (1984): 1689, 1730.

scratch the surface. Indeed, local government in its various forms is today probably more destructive of individual liberty than even the national government.[18]

As long as federalism remains consigned largely to the realm of abstract academic debates, this phenomenon of grassroots tyranny will continue unabated. Yet few legal issues have greater real-world implications than does the question of the proper role of federalism in our society. Indeed, the issue of federalism is in some instances literally a matter of life and death: for better or worse, federalism is a central issue in seminal cases dealing both with abortion and the right to die, and with myriad issues touching our day-to-day lives. If our understanding of federalism and its underlying values remains as hopelessly muddled and confused as it is today, it will leave us at a serious disadvantage in dealing with some of the most bitterly divisive issues that wrack our nation's soul.

"The future of federalism," writes Timothy Conlan, "will ultimately depend on the values that Americans hold in highest esteem."[19] If I am correct in my belief that Americans today value liberty as much as the Framers did, then we must transform federalism from its current status as an impediment to freedom into its intended role as a bulwark of liberty. I hope this book will start that vital process.

---

[18]In a sense, this book is a natural companion volume to Robert Higgs, *Crisis and Leviathan* (New York: Oxford University Press, 1987), which chronicles the tremendous growth of national government.

[19]Timothy Conlan, *New Federalism* (Washington: Brookings Institution, 1988), p. 236.

PART I

FEDERALISM

1. Competing Visions of Federalism

Federalism, wrote Felix Morley in 1959, is "the distinctively American contribution to political art."[1] Indeed, the masterful political artists of America's founding era painted their concept of federalism in bold, crisp, vibrant strokes.

But the years have taken their toll; the colors have faded, the lines have blurred. Little remains of the original product to aid today's observer in discerning the design of the artists.

What is federalism? Like so much in the realm of political art, its meaning lies in the eye of the beholder. So little agreement exists today, in fact, that one scholar of federalism has identified 267 different but overlapping definitions of the term.[2]

Despite all the confusion and disagreement, any serious inquiry into the history and principles of federalism will reveal, as Daniel J. Elazar has observed, that "the central interest of true federalism in all its species is liberty."[3] Liberty is where federalism begins; and, properly understood, liberty is where federalism leads.

As I demonstrate in the following pages, federalism was one of the principal mechanisms that the Framers of the Constitution designed to protect individual liberty. In attempting to create a government capable of preserving nationhood yet at the same time ensuring a free society, they were careful to establish several constitutional devices designed to attain that delicate combination. First, they created a national government of limited and defined powers—the minimum powers necessary for effective government. They also established specific restraints on government power, both in the original Constitution and in the Bill of Rights.

[1]Felix Morley, *Freedom and Federalism* (1959; Indianapolis: Liberty Press, 1981), p. xxiv.

[2]See Timothy Conlan, *New Federalism* (Washington: Brookings Institution, 1988), p. 3.

[3]Daniel J. Elazar, *Exploring Federalism* (Tuscaloosa: University of Alabama Press, 1987), p. 91. Elazar explores in depth the origins and history of the concept of federalism. See pp. 115–52.

The Framers also, as Robert Bork has described it, pursued a "deliberate strategy to create competing centers of power in order to avoid tyranny."[4] Among those were the separation of powers and the system of checks and balances among the three branches of national government. But perhaps most significant from the standpoint of individual liberty was the Framers' adoption of federalism as the operative system of American government. Federalism is the constitutional structure by which government powers are diffused and dispersed as far as is consistent with effective government and fundamental individual liberties. Hence, federalism establishes a constitutional preference for decentralized power, except when it is exercised in a manner adverse to liberty. This design is embodied in the Ninth Amendment, which declares that "the enumeration in the Constitution, of certain rights, shall not be construed to deny or disparage others retained by the people"; and the Tenth Amendment, which says that "the powers not delegated to the United States by the Constitution, nor prohibited by it to the States, are reserved to the States respectively, or to the people."

As reflected by the Tenth Amendment, federalism was designed in part to ensure that the national government remained within the explicitly enumerated powers assigned to it in the Constitution by reserving to the states all other legitimate government powers. But when this provision is read in combination with the Ninth Amendment, it is clear that the preference for state over national government was not perceived as an end in itself, but rather as part of an overall constitutional system designed to preserve individual liberty.

As James Madison emphasized in *The Federalist* no. 46, both states and the national government are agents of the people, and both are bound ultimately by the authority of the people.[5] The Framers intended that individuals retain their natural rights as expressed in the Declaration of Independence, and that the powers possessed by government therefore be limited to those necessary to secure liberty, with individuals retaining all rights not explicitly surren-

[4]Robert H. Bork, *Federalism and Federal Regulation: The Case of Product Labeling* (Washington: Washington Legal Foundation, 1991), p. 1.

[5]*The Federalist* no. 46 (Madison) in *The Federalist Papers* (New York: Modern Library, 1937), pp. 304–5.

dered. This concept of individual sovereignty was central to the Framers' understanding of federalism; without it, remarked James Wilson in the Constitutional Convention, "we shall never be able to understand the principle on which this system was constructed."[6]

The particular apportionment of powers between national and state governments—with the bulk of those powers vested in the states, which were closer to the people—reflected the Framers' calculation of how most effectively to protect individual liberty. Just as the national branches of government were balanced against one another to prevent abuses of rights, so too were the powers of the national and state governments balanced against each other, resulting in what the Framers viewed as "a double security . . . to the rights of the people."[7]

This balance was thrown off during the 19th century, when state governments emerged as the greater threat to individual liberty, particularly in perpetuating the institution of human slavery. In response, the Reconstruction Congress following the Civil War took steps to restrict the ability of state governments to violate individual rights. The Fourteenth Amendment, in particular, granted extensive powers to the national government for the purpose of protecting liberty against deprivations by state governments. The Fourteenth Amendment thus completed the federalism equation: a preference for decentralized power, but only to the extent consistent with the overarching goal of maximizing individual liberty.

In the years since then, few political theorists have maintained fidelity to this original understanding of federalism. Instead, they have tended to choose sides, favoring either national or state power depending upon the desired policy outcome.[8] Contemporary liberals tend to favor national over state power and hence are often viewed as being against federalism, but they also support the power of state and local government when used to regulate the economy and to redistribute wealth and property. Conservatives typically portray themselves as the champions of federalism, but their version of federalism is one that holds as its highest value states' rights rather than individual liberty.

[6]Quoted in Raoul Berger, *Federalism: The Founders' Design* (Norman: University of Oklahoma Press, 1987), p. 52.

[7]*The Federalist* no. 51 (Madison or Hamilton), in *The Federalist Papers*, p. 339.

[8]See Elazar, p. 80.

This conservative/liberal division on the issue of federalism has not always remained consistent. As J. M. Balkin has noted, "states' rights was a *liberal* argument" during the era of economic "substantive due process" early in this century, during which the Supreme Court occasionally struck down state economic regulations as violations of individual liberty and freedom of contract.[9] When Franklin Roosevelt captured the White House and appointed a liberal Supreme Court, the sides switched: liberals favored expansive national power (including the power of federal courts to strike down reactionary state legislation), while conservatives clamored for states' rights as a way of restricting national power.

Nor have either liberals or conservatives gained much consistency in their respective positions on federalism in the years since the New Deal. Liberals often have supported state autonomy when it promotes values they hold dear; conservatives often have tried to override state autonomy in favor of certain social or economic policies at the national level.

Neither group, however, chooses sides in accordance with a consistent preference for individual liberty. Both sides claim to support liberty, but that support depends on the particular liberty involved. As Balkin has explained,

> Neither liberalism nor conservatism is a purely individualist or communalist philosophy. Rather, each position is a melange of individualist and communalist stances on different preferred civil rights. In general, modern liberals are more individualist with respect to free speech, sexual autonomy, and the rights of criminal defendants. They tend to take relatively communalist positions with respect to the right to freedom of contract. Modern conservatives have precisely the opposite orientation.[10]

This selectiveness in preferred liberties, Balkin remarked, "leads to many delightful contradictions in both liberal and conservative ideologies."[11] Such contradictions manifest themselves in internally

[9]J. M. Balkin, "Federalism and the Conservative Ideology," *Urban Lawyer* 19 (1987): 464 (emphasis in original).

[10]Ibid., p. 462.

[11]For an excellent analysis of contemporary political ideologies, see William S. Maddox and Stuart A. Lilie, *Beyond Liberal and Conservative: Reassessing the Political Spectrum* (Washington: Cato Institute, 1984).

inconsistent positions taken by both conservatives and liberals on issues of federalism.

Liberals in recent years have tended to ignore state power as a meaningful restraint on federal power, even if state power is used to protect individual liberty. With liberal domination of the Supreme Court being the case until very recently, the Tenth Amendment's vitality has declined significantly. The emergence of a more conservative Supreme Court, however, has inspired some liberals to rediscover the Tenth Amendment and embrace federalism to protect exercises of state powers designed to further liberal objectives.

Conversely, conservatives have objected strenuously to the Court's preference for national over state power. But like the liberals, their preference for one level of government over another often ignores the more fundamental question of liberty. As Stephen Macedo has aptly observed,

> It is one thing to argue that the federal government has assumed powers reserved to the states, making a mockery of both federalism and a government of enumerated powers. It is quite another thing, and far more difficult, to maintain that the federal government has overstepped its bounds in defending constitutional rights against the states.[12]

Nonetheless, conservatives often do so, and in the process of restraining national power when the ends of such power are illegitimate, they often denigrate the exercise of national power even when applied toward legitimate ends (such as protecting the right to pursue entrepreneurial opportunities against excessive regulation by state governments).

Although both liberals and conservatives often invoke liberty in support of their federalism arguments, in fact neither side evidences anything close to a liberty-based concept of federalism. Instead, federalism issues typically revolve around debates over states' rights.

But the very notion of states' rights is oxymoronic. States don't have rights. States have powers. People have rights. And the primary purpose of federalism is to protect those rights.

---

[12]Stephen Macedo, *The New Right v. the Constitution* (Washington: Cato Institute, 1987), p. 21.

Madison had to deal with this same issue while fighting for ratification of the Constitution, and his insights 200 years ago are precisely on target with respect to the confusion over federalism today:

> The federal and state governments are in fact but different agents and trustees of the people. . . . The adversaries of the Constitution seem to have lost sight of the people altogether in their reasonings on this subject; and to have viewed these different establishments . . . as uncontrolled by any common superior in their efforts to usurp the authorities of each other. These gentlemen must be reminded of their error. They must be told that the ultimate authority . . . resides in the people alone.[13]

This sound counsel is directly applicable to the present confusion surrounding federalism, in which the fundamental principle of individual sovereignty is subordinated, both by conservatives and liberals, to some perceived greater good. Such subordination of the goal of liberty repudiates the intent of the Framers and their understanding of federalism.

We can restore federalism to its intended role as a bulwark of individual liberty only if we confront the errors of those who misapply the principles of federalism, a task that begins with exploring the contemporary debate.

Conservatives: States' Rights Federalism

Modern conservative legal theorists base their conception of the Constitution on the doctrine of original intent. For conservatives, the Framers' intent is paramount, "rising even above the text" in discerning the Constitution's meaning, according to Raoul Berger, the preeminent conservative theorist of federalism.[14]

But Stephen Macedo charges that in practice, the conservative position in many instances "really comes down to . . . the Jurisprudence of Selective Intent," in which the Framers' intent is vindicated "only when the process serves a deeper political commitment—that of construing government powers and the powers of majorities broadly and individual rights narrowly."[15]

---

[13]*The Federalist* no. 46 (Madison), pp. 304–5.

[14]Berger, *Federalism,* p. 16.

[15]Macedo, p. 25.

The modern conservative concept of federalism bolsters Macedo's claim, for conservatives see the central concern of federalism not as individual liberty but rather as states' rights and majoritarianism. They start with an accurate premise—as Berger describes it, the Founders' belief that "the *people* were sovereign"[16]—but they proceed to construct a theory of federalism that subverts individual sovereignty.

Conservatives support this argument by locating the doctrine of federalism almost exclusively in the Tenth Amendment while ignoring altogether the Ninth Amendment, as well as the final clause of the Tenth Amendment, which reserves undelegated powers "to the States respectively, *or to the people*" (emphasis added). Berger's book on federalism, for instance, makes not a single reference to the Ninth Amendment.[17] This emphasis on the Tenth Amendment enables states' rights conservatives to elevate majoritarianism to a constitutional absolute while relegating individual liberty to a tangential role.

Robert Bork, for instance, argues that the Tenth Amendment

> confirms that federal powers were intended to be limited and that the powers not lodged in the national government remained with the states, if the states had such powers under their own constitutions, and, if not, the powers were still held by the people."[18]

But for Bork, the Ninth Amendment presents more of a mystery. At his Supreme Court confirmation hearings, Bork testified,

> I do not think you can use the Ninth Amendment unless you know something of what it means. For example, if you had an amendment that says "Congress shall make no" and then there is an inkblot, and you cannot read the rest of it, . . . I do not think the court can make up what might be under the inkblot.[19]

This curious interpretation is a classic example of selective intent. The Ninth and Tenth Amendments employ similar terms and speak

---

[16]Berger, *Federalism*, p. 44 (emphasis in original).

[17]Ibid., index, pp. 217–23.

[18]Robert H. Bork, *The Tempting of America* (New York: Free Press, 1990), pp. 184–85.

[19]Quoted in *The Rights Retained by the People*, ed. Randy E. Barnett (Fairfax, Va.: George Mason University Press, 1989), p. 1.

in broad generalities. But for Bork, the Tenth Amendment embodies an explicit, readily discernible, and highly sophisticated theory of government, while the Ninth Amendment is an unfathomable ink-blot. Not coincidentally, the language of the Tenth Amendment can be interpreted to support the theory of broad state powers that Bork advocates—but only if read in isolation, as if the Ninth Amendment has no meaning whatsoever.

Bork subsequently has conceded that the Ninth Amendment has some meaning, but only as being redundant of the Tenth Amendment. The Ninth Amendment serves a "parallel" purpose, Bork contends, by "guaranteeing that the rights of the people specified already in the state constitutions were not cast in doubt by the fact that only a limited set of rights was guaranteed by the federal charter."[20] In other words, aside from the handful of rights specifically reserved to the people in the original Constitution (such as the prohibition against ex post facto laws and laws impairing the obligation of contracts), the rights "retained by the people" under the Ninth Amendment consist solely of those that particular states might recognize in their constitutions.

Nor did the Fourteenth Amendment expand this storehouse of rights by "incorporating" the Bill of Rights against the states, according to states' rights conservatives. In 1985, Attorney General Edwin Meese made this view clear in a speech to the American Bar Association, when he declared that "nowhere else has the principle of federalism been dealt so politically violent and constitutionally suspect a blow as by the theory of incorporation."[21]

The constitutional system established by this states' rights construct is composed principally of a broad general rule of state sovereignty, with only two narrow exceptions: the relatively small number of explicitly enumerated powers assigned to the federal government, and the even smaller category of explicitly enumerated rights reserved to the people by their state constitutions or by the federal Constitution. This construct leaves sweeping residual powers in the states, which in the view of states' rights conservatives is exactly

[20]Bork, *The Tempting of America*, p. 185.

[21]Quoted in Michael Kent Curtis, *No State Shall Abridge* (Durham, N.C.: Duke University Press, 1986), p. viii. Curtis makes a compelling case that the Framers of the Fourteenth Amendment intended to incorporate the Bill of Rights against the states under the "privileges or immunities" clause.

the result the Framers intended. "The constitutional doctrine of federalism," contends Bork, requires "leaving the states as sole regulators of areas left beyond federal power."[22] This conception of federalism, argues Lino Graglia, essentially makes state governments "autonomous policymaking entities . . . as to all matters of daily life."[23]

Stephen Macedo counters that

> when conservatives like Bork treat rights as islands surrounded by a sea of government powers, they precisely reverse the view of the Founders as enshrined in the Constitution, wherein government powers are . . . rendered as islands surrounded by a sea of individual rights."[24]

The conservatives facilitate this revisionism by viewing the creation of the Constitution not as an act of individuals forming a "social contract," but as the act of independent, sovereign states.[25] This vision confuses process—the ratification of the Constitution by the states—with purpose. For, as the Declaration of Independence made clear, the goal of the battle for American independence was the rights of the people.

Still, states' rights conservatives strive to maintain the fiction that their view of federalism is consistent with principles of individual autonomy. The "protection of individual liberty," Bork asserts, is "an important benign aspect" of federalism, for it allows states to protect liberties as extensively as they wish. It also allows them to restrict liberty as much as they wish; but this is not a cause for alarm, Bork assures us, because "if another state allows the liberty you value, you can move there."[26]

What about the premise, accepted even by states' rights conservatives, that ultimate sovereignty resides in the people? The conservatives accommodate this premise by viewing individual sovereignty

[22]Bork, *The Tempting of America*, p. 52.

[23]Lino A. Graglia, "Restoring the Federalist System: How to Return Control of Local Affairs to Local Authority," unpublished manuscript prepared for the Advisory Commission on Intergovernmental Relations, pp. 2–3.

[24]Macedo, p. 32.

[25]Berger, *Federalism*, p. 26. Here, Berger explicitly rejects the statement by Justice Joseph Story that the union "was emphatically the act of the whole people of the united colonies."

[26]Bork, *The Tempting of America*, pp. 52–53.

not in the usual sense of the term—that is, the ability of individuals to conduct their own affairs free from coercive interference—but rather in terms of what Raoul Berger calls "their right to self-government."[27] These may sound like the same thing, but they're not: self-government as understood by states' rights conservatives does not mean individual liberty, but majoritarianism.[28] In other words, the right of self-government means the right to limit the liberty of others through majoritarian processes. By clothing states' rights federalism in this conceptual facade of self-government, conservatives thus can assert that their concept of federalism protects individual autonomy even as it subverts precious individual liberties.

Under this construct, no liberties are secure, in that individuals are entitled to liberties only when they are granted by particular state constitutions. Hence, an individual's asserted right to be free from coercive interferences is entitled to no greater weight than another individual's right to impose such coercion, with either "right" existing only if it is derived from the right of self-government as effectuated through majoritarian processes. In Bork's words: "Every clash between a minority claiming freedom and a majority claiming power to regulate involves a choice between the gratifications of two groups."[29] Because no principled basis exists to choose between the competing gratifications, Bork submits, the power to choose ought to reside in the majority.[30] After all, claims Bork, "the original Constitution was devoted primarily to the mechanisms of democratic choice," which requires those who believe in original intent to reject any "theory that removes from democratic control areas of life the framers intended to leave there."[31]

The genius of federalism, according to states' rights conservatives, is that it vests the greatest government powers in precisely the forum that is most likely to satisfy majoritarian will—the states.

[27]Raoul Berger, "The Ninth Amendment," in Barnett, p. 218.

[28]See discussion on this point in Macedo, pp. 26, 88.

[29]Robert H. Bork, "Neutral Principles and Some First Amendment Problems," *Indiana Law Journal* 47 (1971): 9–11.

[30]Ibid.

[31]Robert H. Bork, *Tradition and Morality in Constitutional Law* (Washington: American Enterprise Institute for Public Policy Research, 1984), pp. 8–9.

As Graglia observes, "the smaller the decision unit, the fewer the number of people whose preferences will be rejected."[32]

But the Framers also recognized that the facility of small governments in accommodating the gratifications of majorities could be a double-edged sword, in that unrestrained majoritarianism could lead to abuses of the rights of minorities (and of the minority of one, the individual). Pointing to *The Federalist* no. 10, Judge Alex Kozinski noted that "the Founding Fathers recognized [that] the narrower a government's domain, the greater the likelihood of oppression."[33]

Given this recognition that abuses of rights could occur even in the smallest of governments, the Framers were not concerned primarily with favoring one type of government over another, but with *limiting the power of government*, regardless of its source. This understanding is lost on modern states' rights conservatives, who view federalism as a preference for the power of state governments over the national government, with the question of individual sovereignty being subsumed within the ambit of states' rights.

To put this proposition another way, the states' rights conservatives perceive state power as an expression of, or proxy for, individual sovereignty; hence they assume that state power and individual sovereignty are necessarily coincidental.[34] They therefore see issues of federalism exclusively in terms of conflicts between the Tenth Amendment on the one hand, and exercises of national power (typically under either the commerce clause or the Fourteenth

[32]Graglia, p. 1.

[33]*Associated General Contractors of California* v. *City & County of San Francisco*, 813 F.2d 922, 929 (9th Cir. 1987).

[34]Even so strong an advocate of individual liberty as Felix Morley committed this error. He argued, for instance, that the Fourteenth Amendment—which was intended to protect individual liberty against abuses of power by state governments—"has proved invidious to the strength of federalism in the United States." Morley, p. 88; see generally ibid., pp. 76–92. The explanation lies apparently in that Morley's book was written in 1959, with the recent experience of the New Deal fresh in mind and with the enormous further expansion of national power by the federal judiciary taking place as the book was being written. After 27 years of steady expansion of national power, often at the expense of individual liberties, one could easily assume that the interests of state governments and individual liberties were coincidental.

Amendment) on the other.[35] In this battle, they tend instinctively to favor state autonomy, regardless of where it leads. In the states' rights construct, however, this constant preference for state power is not inconsistent with general conservative notions of individual liberty, in that the essence of that liberty is the right to self-government as expressed through state and local governments.

As state powers are broadened under this construct, individual liberties necessarily are constrained. This attachment to states' rights as an end in itself often leads conservatives to resist judicial protection for liberties they ordinarily favor in the policy arena (such as economic liberty),[36] but it also allows them to deny protection to liberties they do not support (such as the right to privacy). That produces an internal consistency of a sort, for it means that conservatives generally disfavor altogether judicial protection of individual liberty, at least invoked against the exercise of state power. Once again, conservatives see no contradiction with the Framers' determination to protect individual liberty, in that, as Bork explains, "the major freedom . . . of our kind of society is the freedom to choose to have a public morality."[37] Because majoritarianism is the paramount value under our Constitution, other liberties must give way to the democratically established public morality. As Bork argues,

> Liberties that are deeply rooted in our history and tradition . . . must be matters the Founders left to the legislature, either because they assumed no legislature would be mad enough to do away with them or because they wished to allow the legislature discretion to regulate the area as they saw fit."[38]

[35]Berger, *Federalism*, p. 20. Berger identifies other primary sources of conflict in the national government's powers under the Constitution's "necessary and proper," "supremacy," and "general welfare" clauses.

[36]See Balkin, p. 489.

[37]Bork, *Tradition and Morality in Constitutional Law*, p. 9. Bork did not always feel that way. In 1963, he assailed the proposed Civil Rights Act as "legislation by which the morals of the majority are self-righteously imposed upon a minority. That has happened before in the United States—Prohibition being the most notorious instance—but whenever it happens it is likely to be subversive of free institutions." See Robert Bork, "Civil Rights—A Challenge," *The New Republic*, August 31, 1963, p. 21.

[38]Bork, *The Tempting of America*, p. 119.

24

Should anyone misunderstand the implications of this doctrine, Bork makes his point even clearer. Referring to *Lochner* v. *New York*,[39] a major economic liberty opinion early in this century, Bork declares that "Justice Peckham, defending liberty from what he conceived to be 'a mere meddlesome interference,' asked rhetorically, '[A]re we all   at the mercy of legislative majorities?' The correct answer, where the Constitution is silent, must be 'yes.' "[40]

Applying this philosophy, Edwin Meese in 1985 attacked the Supreme Court for certain decisions in which it used the equal protection clause of the Fourteenth Amendment to curb "state power to regulate the economy," while lauding "the respect shown . . . for state and local sovereignty" in cases in which the Court upheld anticompetitive acts against antitrust challenges.[41] In each of these cases, Meese sided with state and local governments that were restricting economic liberty—the freedom to make contracts or to participate in the marketplace. Like Bork, Meese viewed such losses of liberty as serving a higher value. "By allowing the States sovereignty to govern," explained Meese, "we better secure our ultimate goal of political liberty through decentralized government."[42]

Meese's statement summarizes the conception of federalism held by states' rights conservatives. It is one in which majoritarianism is elevated to a constitutional absolute, and in which precious individual liberties are subordinated to group or societal rights, variously described as "political liberty," "the right to self-government," or the right to establish a "public morality." Though grounded in a profound distrust of national power, the conservative theory of federalism has as its primary effect the enlargement of government power at state and local levels. As Attorney General

[39]198 U.S. 45 (1905).

[40]Bork, *The Tempting of America*, p. 49.

[41]Edwin Meese III, speech before the American Bar Association, in *The Great Debate: Interpreting Our Written Constitution* (Washington: Federalist Society, 1986), p. 1. Attorney General Meese criticized the Supreme Court's rulings in *Metropolitan Life Insurance Co.* v. *Ward*, 470 U.S. 869 (1985) and *Supreme Court of New Hampshire* v. *Piper*, 470 U.S. 274 (1985); he endorsed its decisions in *Town of Hallie* v. *City of Eau Claire*, 471 U.S. 34 (1985) and *Southern Motor Carriers Rate Conference* v. *United States*, 471 U.S. 48 (1985).

[42]Meese, speech before the American Bar Association, p. 5.

Meese aptly remarked in a different context, "The essence of federalism is the protection of liberty."[43] But this essence is largely absent—indeed subverted—in the states' rights concept of federalism. By constructing a rationale for unbounded state power within the rubric of federalism, states' rights conservatives have opened the jurisprudential floodgates to a regime of grassroots tyranny.

Liberals: Social Action Federalism

For contemporary liberals, federalism is a recent discovery. Whereas previous liberal jurisprudence consigned federalism to the dustbin of history, today's liberals often find federalism a hospitable doctrine with which to defend their policy innovations at the state and local levels. Like conservatives, however, liberals clothe their concept of federalism in sympathetic rhetoric, but do not always invoke federalism in the service of individual liberty.

At least since the New Deal, liberals have tended to disparage federalism, and it was liberal jurisprudence that reduced the Tenth Amendment to a mere constitutional "truism."[44] But with the recent emergence of a conservative majority on the Supreme Court—with its frequent preference for state over national power and its disinclination to advance the liberal political agenda—liberals have discovered the usefulness of federalism, or at least a federalism shaped toward their own ends.

Liberals employ considerable license in imputing to the Framers a concept of federalism that accommodates the liberal agenda. "Federalism preserves the states," declares Robert H. Freilich, "not for the purpose of diluting the power of the national government in domestic issues or of overriding minority interests in our society, but of encouraging creativity in government."[45] One would be hard-pressed to find much in the way of constitutional history to reveal a serious interest in government "creativity" on the part of the Framers, but that does not deter liberals from trying to make it the linchpin of federalism.

[43]Quoted in Michael Kammen, *Sovereignty and Liberty* (Madison: University of Wisconsin Press, 1988), p. 196.

[44]*United States* v. *Darby*, 312 U.S. 100, 124 (1940).

[45]Robert H. Freilich, "A Proposed Congressional 'Statute of Federalism,' " *Urban Lawyer* 19 (1987): 539, 541–42.

Social action, or experimental, federalism traces its origins to early 20th century jurisprudence, when the Supreme Court was dominated by conservatives who sometimes struck down economic regulations as violations of individual liberty. In its 1932 decision in *New State Ice Co.* v. *Liebmann,* for instance, the Court invalidated an Oklahoma law that forbade the manufacture or sale of ice without a showing of public necessity and consent by a state regulatory board. "The principle is embedded in our constitutional system," declared Justice George Sutherland for the Court's majority, "that there are certain essentials of liberty with which the state is not entitled to dispense in the interest of experiments." The Court also rejected the argument that some rights were entitled to greater protection than others. Sutherland noted that only a year earlier, "the theory of experimentation in censorship was not permitted to interfere with the fundamental doctrine of the freedom of the press. The opportunity to apply one's labor and skill in an ordinary occupation . . . is no less entitled to protection."[46]

But Justice Louis Brandeis dissented, articulating a rationale for social action federalism:

> There must be power in the States . . . to remould, through experimentation, our economic practices to meet changing social and economic needs. . . . It is one of the happy incidents of the federal system that a single courageous State may, if its citizens choose, serve as a laboratory.[47]

The views expressed by Brandeis would, of course, prevail within a few years, as the Supreme Court upheld expansive New Deal legislation adopted by all levels of government.

The leading contemporary theorist and proponent of liberal federalism is former justice William Brennan. As a member of the Court, Brennan was instrumental both in shaping the liberal response to states' rights federalism and in fashioning the concept of social action federalism.

Brennan's views on federalism evolved as the requirements of the liberal political agenda changed. "Although Justice Brennan

---

[46]*New State Ice Co.* v. *Liebmann,* 285 U.S. 262, 280 (1932), citing *Near* v. *Minnesota,* 283 U.S. 697 (1931).

[47]Ibid., p. 311 (Brandeis, J., dissenting).

describes himself as a 'devout believer' in the concept of federalism," charges Earl M. Maltz, "his judicial record suggests otherwise."[48] Maltz correctly observes that "Brennan apparently defines 'healthy' federalism as a system which enforces the values with which he agrees."[49]

These preferred values are those that were in ascendancy during the Supreme Court's Warren era, roughly from the mid-1950s until the early 1970s, in which the Court expanded protection of certain vital individual liberties (particularly freedom of speech and the right to privacy), but in which it also broadened protections for criminal defendants, beneficiaries of social welfare entitlements, and racial groups (as opposed to individual members of those groups).[50] Once the Supreme Court ceased to consistently advance those values, Brennan perceived a broader role for the states to do so. But for Brennan, the primary actors in this social action species of federalism are not the legislatures, but the courts. "Given the minimal importance of state autonomy as a value in his decisions," remarks Maltz, "Justice Brennan's appeal to the concept of federalism must reflect a belief that state court activism will advance some other set of values."[51] Brennan's "true agenda," Maltz charges, is that "state courts should vindicate personal liberties along the lines undertaken by the Warren Court."[52]

Brennan's record on federalism supports Maltz's thesis. Typically, when a case involved a clash between national regulatory power and the states' efforts to resist it, Brennan sided with the national government, even if it meant a diminution of individual liberty. But when the national government sought to constrain state regulation directed toward liberal ends—such as affirmative action or restrictions of private property rights—Brennan generally defended state autonomy.

Brennan's enthusiasm for federalism grew as the Supreme Court's support for Warren-era values eroded. In 1964, Brennan

[48]Earl M. Maltz, "False Prophet—Justice Brennan and the Theory of State Constitutional Law," *Hastings Constitutional Law Quarterly* 15 (1988): 429, 430.

[49]Ibid., p. 433.

[50]See, for example, Clint Bolick, *Changing Course: Civil Rights at the Crossroads* (New Brunswick, N.J.: Transaction Books, 1988), pp. 60–74.

[51]Maltz, p. 432.

[52]Ibid.

called upon state courts to broadly construe federal law, arguing that "the fundamental obligation to administer federal law rests on both [federal and state] courts," which properly possess an "identity of underlying purpose."[53] But by 1977, when the Supreme Court no longer was interpreting federal law broadly in all cases, Brennan was urging state courts to broadly interpret their own constitutions. Brennan declared that

> state courts cannot rest when they have afforded their citizens the full protections of the federal Constitution. State constitutions, too, are a font of individual liberties, their protections often extending beyond those required by the Supreme Court's interpretation of federal law. The legal revolution which has brought federal law to the fore must not be allowed to inhibit the independent protective force of state law. . . .[54]

Concluded Brennan, "Every believer in our concept of federalism, and I am a devout believer, must salute this development in our state courts" to broadly construe state constitutional provisions.[55]

Brennan constructed an elaborate rationale to advance his newfound concept of federalism. Much of his rhetoric sounds remarkably sympathetic to the Framers' desire to protect individual liberty. "Federalism," said Brennan, "need not be a mean-spirited doctrine that serves only to limit the scope of human liberty."[56] The Constitution, Brennan argued, is "a blueprint for government. And when the text is not prescribing the form of government, it is limiting the powers of that government." Ultimately, Brennan declared, the Constitution defines "the relationship of the individual and the state," and embodies "a sparkling vision of the supremacy of the human dignity of every individual."[57] Such a Constitution is incompatible with unconstrained majoritarianism. Said Brennan, "It is the very purpose of a Constitution—and particularly of the Bill of

---

[53]William J. Brennan, Jr., "Some Aspects of Federalism," *New York University Law Review* 39 (1964): 945, 959.

[54]William J. Brennan, Jr., "State Constitutions and the Protection of Individual Rights," *Harvard Law Review* 90 (1977): 489, 491.

[55]Ibid., p. 502.

[56]Ibid., p. 503.

[57]William J Brennan, Jr., speech given at Georgetown University (1985), in *The Great Debate*, p. 18.

Rights—to declare certain values transcendent, beyond the reach of temporary political majorities."[58]

Where Brennan veered off course was in his definition of liberty. Sometimes, particularly in First Amendment cases, Brennan spoke of liberty in its ordinary (and constitutional) meaning of freedom from arbitrary constraints imposed by government. But his broader view was of a constitution that "embodies the aspiration to social justice" and "egalitarianism."[59] Hence, Brennan regularly supported state power to impose racial quotas or to redistribute private property against assertions of federal constitutional rights. The individual liberties protected by Brennan's concept of federalism are thus highly selective.

Liberals are correct when they argue that federalism can play an important role in protecting liberty, but in practice the liberal brand of federalism is often destructive of individual liberty. As Virginia Postrel argues, liberal state activism

> works in one direction: toward bigger government and more restrictive regulation. States aren't allowed to pass lower minimum wages, weaker environmental controls, or simpler labeling laws than the federal government. But, unless otherwise specified, they can always pass more stringent laws.[60]

The semantic gymnastics employed by proponents of social action federalism thus underscore the need for true proponents of a liberty-based theory of federalism to define liberty carefully and precisely. (Such a theory is presented in the next two chapters.)

Missing the Point: The Federalism Debate Today

The Framers probably would delight in the notion that federalism remains a vibrant topic of public policy debate more than 200 years

---

[58]Ibid., p. 16. Curiously, Brennan observed that "unabashed enshrinement of majority will would permit . . . wholesale confiscation of property so long as a majority of the authorized legislative body, fairly elected, approved. Our Constitution could not abide such a situation." Ibid. I am not aware of any cases following this 1985 speech in which Brennan viewed the destruction of private-property rights as unconstitutional under such circumstances.

[59]Ibid.

[60]Virginia I. Postrel, "The States Are Becoming the New 'Big Government,' " *Washington Post*, July 14, 1991, p. C3.

after the American experiment was launched. But they likely would despair over the lack of modern understanding of the purposes of federalism. Indeed, the most notable aspect of the contemporary debate over federalism, on both ends of the political spectrum, is the almost total absence of serious discussion or concern about individual liberty.

Contemporary federalism jurisprudence is exemplified by two landmark cases, *National League of Cities* v. *Usery*[61] and *Garcia* v. *San Antonio Metropolitan Transit Authority*,[62] in which the liberal/conservative argument over national power versus states' rights played out according to form.

In the 1976 *National League of Cities* case, the Supreme Court confronted an attempt by Congress to extend the minimum-wage and maximum-hours provisions of the Fair Labor Standards Act to employees of state governments and their subdivisions. Thus was presented a choice between the power of the national government to regulate employer/employee relationships on one hand, and the right of state governments and their employees to freely bargain over the terms and conditions of employment on the other.

But Justice William Rehnquist, writing for a 5-4 majority, viewed the issue solely in terms of state sovereignty under the Tenth Amendment. He crafted a rule that regulation by the national government of traditional state functions violates the principles of federalism. Rather than buttressing his decision by noting the federal law's interference with individual liberty, he explicitly repudiated any liberty-based notion of federalism. In fact, he declared, the decision would be altogether different if the congressional regulation were addressed to individuals rather than to the states as such. "It is one thing to recognize the authority of Congress to enact laws regulating individual businesses," he stated, but "it is quite another to uphold a similar exercise of congressional authority directed, not to private citizens, but to the States as States."[63] In other words, national regulation of economic activities is permissible, no matter how extensive or injurious; but national regulation

[61]426 U.S. 833 (1976).
[62]469 U.S. 528 (1985).
[63]*National League of Cities*, at 845.

of traditional state functions is impermissible, no matter how important its purpose or insubstantial its effect.

By divorcing federalism from any concern with individual liberty, Rehnquist allowed the liberal dissenters to attack him from that perspective. Were this a case raising claims of individual liberty, Brennan advised, it might present a more difficult issue in that the Bill of Rights protects specific liberties that the national "commerce power may not infringe." However, declared Brennan, "there is no restraint based on state sovereignty requiring or permitting judicial enforcement anywhere expressed in the Constitution."[64]

By "differentiating 'the people' from 'the States' " and protecting the states but not the people from exercises of the national commerce power, Brennan charged, the majority was crafting a concept of state sovereignty "consonant with their view of a proper distribution of governmental power" but in "defiance of the plain language of the Tenth Amendment."[65] In Brennan's view, however, the Tenth Amendment protects neither state powers nor individual liberty against infringements by the federal government. "Nothing in the Tenth Amendment," Brennan contended, "constitutes a limitation on congressional exercise of powers delegated by the Constitution to Congress."[66] Instead, "restraints upon exercise by Congress of its plenary commerce power lie in the political process and not in the judicial process," insisted Brennan—expressing a view more than a bit like Robert Bork's with respect to state powers.

The difference between the conservative view represented by Bork and the liberal view of Brennan thus lies not in one or the other's consistent support for individual liberty, but in their respective preferences for which level of government may with impunity compromise that liberty. For Bork it's the states, for Brennan it's usually the national government. Either way, liberty stands unprotected in all but passing rhetoric.

That dichotomy surfaced again nine years later when the Court overturned its *National League of Cities* ruling in *Garcia*, a decision conservatives revile as a fundamental repudiation of federalism. In *Garcia*, a metropolitan transit authority sought exemption from the

---

[64]Ibid., at 858 (Brennan, J., dissenting).
[65]Ibid., at 869 n. 9.
[66]Ibid., at 862.

provisions of the Fair Labor Standards Act. Under its *National League of Cities* doctrine, the Court's decision would have turned on whether public transportation was a traditional state government function; but in *Garcia*, a 5-4 majority discarded that standard as unworkable, embracing Brennan's dissent in *National League of Cities* as the new rule of law and thereby upholding the federal regulation.

Like the conservative majority in *National League of Cities*, the liberal majority in *Garcia* cast the issue in terms of national versus state power. But in order to choose national over state power, the majority repudiated the Framers' constitutional vision of a national government of finite, enumerated powers. The commerce power, the majority concluded, was essentially limitless, subject to constraint only through ordinary political processes. "With rare exceptions," Justice Harry Blackmun wrote for the majority, "the Constitution does not carve out express elements of state sovereignty that Congress may not employ its delegated powers to displace."[67] Instead, wrote Blackmun, "the principal and basic limit on the federal commerce power is that inherent in all congressional action—the built-in restraints that our system provides through state participation in federal government action."[68] States enjoy an influential role in this process, reasoned the majority: In addition to representation of the states as such in the Senate, the states influence the actions of the national government through the electoral college's selection of the president and by their power to set qualifications for federal offices. The fact that these influences are indirect and unlikely to halt congressional action that might harm state prerogatives in any given instance was apparently of little moment to the *Garcia* majority. Nor did the challenged law's impact on individual liberty give the majority pause.

The liberals' reasoning in *Garcia* hoist the conservatives on their own majoritarian petard. The conservatives on the Court were aghast at the notion that states could protect their "rights" only through the political process, even though they have no such concern with respect to assertions of individual rights against authoritarian state laws. That raises a significant question: What makes

[67] *Garcia*, at 550.
[68] Ibid., at 556.

states' rights more important—or less protectable within the political process—than individual rights? Once the conservatives removed federalism from its foundation in individual liberty, they jettisoned the only principled basis on which to establish any meaningful structural limits on national government power.

Perhaps sensing this, Justice Lewis Powell's dissent in *Garcia* relied heavily on federalism's central role in protecting liberty. Indeed, Powell's dissent is one of the most cogent contemporary explications of the constitutional doctrine of federalism.

The Court's ruling, charged Powell, "effectively reduces the Tenth Amendment to meaningless rhetoric,"[69] an outcome he viewed as tragic in that "judicial enforcement of the Tenth Amendment is essential to maintaining the federal system so carefully designed by the Framers."[70] That system consisted of a national government of defined powers and dealing primarily with war and foreign commerce, and state governments possessing all additional powers. As Powell emphasized, "The Framers believed that the separate sphere of sovereignty reserved to the States would serve as an effective 'counterpoise' to the power of the Federal Government."[71] But "by usurping functions traditionally performed by the States," Powell declared, "federal overreaching under the Commerce Clause undermines the constitutionally mandated balance of powers between the States and the Federal Government, a balance designed to protect our fundamental liberties."[72]

This balance is destroyed—and liberty compromised—when no limit other than the political process is placed on the power of the national government. As Powell concluded, the effect of the majority's decision is that "federal political officials, invoking the Commerce Clause, are the sole judges of the limits of their own power," a result "inconsistent with the fundamental principles of our constitutional system."[73]

Powell's stinging dissent unmasked the liberals' support for virtually unlimited national regulatory power over economic affairs,

[69]Ibid., at 560 (Powell, J., dissenting).
[70]Ibid., at 570.
[71]Ibid., at 571.
[72]Ibid., at 572.
[73]Ibid., at 567.

despite the deleterious impact of such regulation on individual liberty. But it came too late to make a difference. The Court's shifting majority in *Garcia* sounded the death knell for the Tenth Amendent. Any libertarian function the amendment might have served was thus abandoned along with the liberal majority's repudiation of the rationale of states' rights—a rationale that, by itself, was in any event inadequate to serve as a viable safeguard against abuses of national power.

Justice Rehnquist, in a separate *Garcia* dissent, declared that the rule of law in *National League of Cities* "will, I am confident, in time again command the support of a majority of this Court."[74] Indeed, recent civil rights and criminal habeas corpus rulings decided in favor of states on federalism grounds suggest the conservatives may now have enough votes to overturn *Garcia*.[75] But if they do, will it make a difference? As long as the lines are drawn in terms of national versus state power, with little or no regard for the underlying purpose of federalism to protect individual liberty, neither side can hope to consistently hold the moral high ground or to faithfully effectuate the Framers' intent.

In a sense, although neither side in the contemporary debate over federalism has it completely right, both sides have part of it right. As Attorney General Meese aptly observed, *Garcia* contravenes "the Framers' intention that state and local governments be a buffer against the centralizing tendencies of the national leviathan."[76] On the other hand, the liberals were correct in stating in *Garcia* that the line drawn in *National League of Cities*—a blanket exemption of traditional state functions from federal regulation—was unworkable.

Of course that line is unworkable. It was drawn in the wrong place. It ignores where the Framers intended to draw the line, which was in favor of decentralized authority as a step toward the ultimate objective of maximizing individual autonomy. Sometimes it happens that the exercise of national power is necessary to protect

---

[74]Ibid., at 580 (Rehnquist, J., dissenting).

[75]See, for example, *Gregory* v. *Ashcroft*, 59 U.S.L.W. 4714 (June 18, 1991), and *Coleman* v. *Thompson*, 59 U.S.L.W. 4789 (June 25, 1991). As if to underscore the shift on the Court, Justice Sandra Day O'Connor began her majority opinion in *Coleman* with the words, "This is a case about federalism." Ibid., p. 4790.

[76]Meese, p. 3.

individual liberty, and such a result is not inconsistent with federalism. But other times, as in *Garcia*, protecting state autonomy is necessary to protect individual liberty.

In the final analysis, then, both sides have it wrong. Liberals such as Brennan, in their desire to maximize the regulatory power of the national government, display a cavalier disregard for the concept of federalism and the values it embodies even as they selectively champion individual liberty. Conservatives such as Bork confuse the concept of federalism by emphasizing states' rights as the ultimate objective, thereby leaving federalism vulnerable to attack and to disrepute.

The only solution is to rediscover and reinvigorate the principles of federalism, to explore their origin and their meaning, and to apply those principles to contemporary realities.

2. Federalism in the Grand Design

When the Framers of the Constitution set about the task of form-ing a new system of government for our fledgling nation, they faced a daunting task. Under the Articles of Confederation, the government seemed incapable of managing the country's affairs. The loose federation structure had encouraged 13 highly indepen-dent states to think of themselves as sovereign entities and not as part of a unified nation. The challenge presented to the Framers was to transform this cacophony into harmony without sacrificing the principles over which the American Revolution had been fought.

The Framers had three seemingly irreconcilable goals: to create a national government with sufficient powers to govern effectively, to convince the states to surrender as much of their autonomy as necessary to accomplish the first goal, and to achieve all of this while providing durable safeguards for individual liberty. The Framers set forth their goals in the preamble to the Constitution, declaring the new system of government necessary "in Order to form a more perfect Union, establish Justice, insure domestic Tranquility, pro-vide for the common defence, promote the general Welfare, and secure the Blessings of Liberty to ourselves and our Posterity."

Fresh from the experience of monarchical oppression, the Fram-ers were united in their distrust of a strong central government, and they viewed the states as being essential to the preservation of liberty. Edward S. Corwin has observed that the Revolution was "a contest for local autonomy as well as one for individual liberty."[1] These two objectives, in his words, were "less competitive than complementary," in that the experience of colonial America had

---

[1]Edward S. Corwin, "The 'Higher Law' Background of American Constitutional Law," in *The Rights Retained by the People*, ed. Randy E. Barnett (Fairfax, Va.: George Mason University Press, 1989), pp. 83–84.

demonstrated that "the best protection of the rights of the individual was to be found in the maintenance of the hard-won prerogatives of the colonial legislatures against the royal governors."[2] Indeed, the large majority of states either had enacted protections for individual rights in their constitutions or had adopted separate bills of rights.[3]

This view of the states as guardians of individual liberty did not diminish with efforts to establish a stronger national government, and indeed it was one of the principal assumptions upon which the concept of federalism was based. As James Madison declared, even "the greatest opponents to a Federal Government admit the State Legislatures to be sure guardians of the people's liberty."[4] Justice Lewis F. Powell would later observe that "the Framers recognized that the most effective democracy occurs at local levels of government, where people with firsthand knowledge of local problems have more ready access to public officials responsible for dealing with them."[5]

But the Framers also recognized the potential for state governments to engage in tyranny. "The smaller the society," Madison remarked, "the smaller the number of individuals composing a majority, and . . . the more easily will they concert and execute their plans of oppression."[6] Indeed, one failing of the Articles of Confederation was the inability of the national government to prevent abuses of individual liberty inflicted by state governments. Some states, for instance, had enacted protectionist laws that impeded freedom of commerce among individuals in different states.[7] "The great and radical vice in the construction of the existing Confederation," charged Alexander Hamilton, "is in the principle

---

[2]Ibid.

[3]David A. Logan, "Judicial Federalism in the Court of History" *Oregon Law Review* 66 (1988): 453, 467 n. 68.

[4]James Madison, "Speech to the House Explaining His Proposed Amendment and His Notes for the Amendment Speech," in Barnett, ed., *The Rights Retained by the People*, p. 61.

[5]*Garcia* v. *San Antonio Metropolitan Transit Authority*, 469 U.S. 528, 575 n. 18 (1985)(Powell, J., dissenting).

[6]*The Federalist* no. 10 (Madison), in *The Federalist Papers* (New York: Modern Library, 1937), pp. 60–61.

[7]Logan, p. 459.

of legislation for states or governments, in their corporate or collective capacities, and as contradistinguished from the individuals of which they consist."[8] This occasional tendency of states to succumb to majoritarian tyranny was one of the motivations to create a stronger national government. Because the broader scope of a national government makes it more difficult for special interests to manipulate power for their own ends, Madison reasoned that the superior ability to guard against such abuses would be "enjoyed by the Union over the States composing it."[9]

The Framers thus understood that state governments could at once stand both as bulwarks of liberty and as oppressors of liberty. Accordingly, they determined not to favor one level of government over another, but instead to provide stronger protections for individual liberty against tyranny by government at any level. The core value was liberty; the seminal threat to that value was government in all its forms.

Indeed, the greatest threat to liberty, the Framers believed, was from the people themselves. The desire to prevent popular majorities from using the coercive power of government to tyrannize the minority was a major and recurrent theme in arguments in favor of the Constitution. As Madison warned in a letter to Thomas Jefferson,

> Wherever the real power in a Government lies, there is the danger of oppression. In our Governments the real power lies in the majority of the Community, and the invasion of private rights is chiefly to be apprehended, not from acts of Government contrary to the sense of its constituents, but from acts in which the Government is the mere instrument of the major number of the Constituents.[10]

Hence, Madison urged not a system in which protection of liberty was entrusted to any particular government entity, but one in which liberty was protected against infringements regardless of their source. "The prescriptions in favor of liberty ought to be levelled

[8]*The Federalist* no. 15 (Hamilton), in *The Federalist Papers*, p. 89.

[9]*The Federalist* no. 10 (Madison), p. 61.

[10]Quoted in Randy E. Barnett, "James Madison's Ninth Amendment," in Barnett, ed., *The Rights Retained by the People*, p. 21.

against that quarter where the greatest danger lies," declared Madison. "But this is not found in either the Executive or Legislative departments of Government, but in the body of the people, operating by the majority against the minority."[11]

Such instances of majoritarian tyranny would be advanced through the emergence of "factions," which Madison defined as "a number of citizens . . . who are united and actuated by some common impulse of passion, or of interest, adverse to the rights of other citizens, or to the permanent and aggregate interests of the community."[12] To preserve liberty, Madison warned, factions "must be rendered . . . unable to concert and carry into effect schemes of oppression."[13]

Thus, for Madison, "To secure the public good and private rights against the danger of such a faction, and at the same time to preserve the spirit and the form of popular government" were the "great object" of republican government.[14] To accomplish that object, observed Felix Morley, the Founders "devised a balanced political structure, designed to protect minorities against the majority, right down to that minority of one, the individual."[15] Federalism, which balances the national government against the states and limits the powers of both, is an integral part of the overall political structure calculated to maximize individual liberty within the framework of effective government.

The Crafting of Federalism

The principal purpose of the Constitution was to strengthen the national government. As set forth in the preamble, certain government functions, such as providing for the common defense, were deemed especially suited to unified and centralized enforcement and administration. But in forging such a new system of government, the Framers encountered substantial skepticism and hostility

---

[11]Quoted in *The Great Debate: Interpreting Our Written Constitution* (Washington: Federalist Society, 1986), p. 16.

[12]*The Federalist* no. 10 (Madison), p. 54.

[13]Ibid., p. 58.

[14]Ibid., pp. 57–58.

[15]Felix Morley, *Freedom and Federalism* (1959; Indianapolis: Liberty Press, 1981), p. 31.

among many who believed that a strong central government necessarily would compromise or negate the principles over which the
American Revolution had been waged.

Most of the opposition to a stronger national government took
either or both of two forms. Many critics resisted the diminution of
state powers that inevitably would result from conferring additional
powers to the central government. Others viewed a strengthened
national government as a threat to liberty. These two "antifederal-
ist" arguments (as previously noted) were often perceived as two
sides of the same coin, in that the states were viewed as the most
reliable guardians of liberty.

But many who supported a stronger national government—the
advocates of the new proposed Constitution, known as federalists[16]—did so precisely because they viewed the states as inadequate protectors of liberty, particularly when the states' parochial
interests conflicted with the rights of individuals. As Robert Hawkins has observed, both sides had similar concerns. The antifederal-
ists opposed a strong national government "on the basis that the
smaller state governments would be more responsive to their citizens and more controllable."[17] But federalists feared that "smaller
governments would more likely be controlled by a strong majority
. . . and would more likely oppress [their] minorities," as Madison
argued in *The Federalist* no. 10.[18]

---

[16]The term "federalists" as used to describe those who supported a stronger
national government has generated endless confusion, in that federalism generally
is taken to mean support for local or state autonomy. Today's federalists generally
oppose expansive national power. The adoption of the term by the proponents of
the Constitution was not accidental. As John M. Murrin has observed, "Because
the authors of the new government called themselves 'Federalists,' their annoyed
opponents found themselves stuck with the label of 'Anti-Federalists,' even though
the adjective 'federal' had always implied decentralization of power." John M.
Murrin, "1787: The Invention of American Federalism," in *Essays on Liberty and
Federalism*, ed. David E. Narrett (College Station: Texas A&M University Press,
1988), p. 40.

[17]Robert B. Hawkins, Jr., "Federalism: The Contemporary Challenge," in *Federalism: The Legacy of George Mason*, ed. Martin B. Cohen (Fairfax, Va.: George Mason
University Press, 1988), p. 105. At the time this work was published, Hawkins
served as chairman of the Advisory Commission on Intergovernmental Relations.

[18]Ibid.

41

Hence, one of the major challenges facing the Framers of the Constitution was to accommodate three disparate and often competing goals: creating a national government with powers sufficient to govern; preserving to the greatest possible extent the powers of state governments; and protecting individual liberty. Federalism was the system they established to strike an appropriate and durable balance among these three objectives.

The Framers created federalism layer by layer. At the core of their concept of federalism was the principle of individual sovereignty.

One of the most vexing issues they encountered was the question of national versus state sovereignty. The Articles of Confederation had established a national government of a sort, but little doubt existed that the powers of the states ultimately were paramount. Under a new Constitution, would this primacy shift to the national government? If so, such a construct might never win assent, given that the Constitution required ratification by state conventions. On the other hand, any system of government that vested ultimate sovereignty in the states would inevitably produce a national government incapable of governing. Complicating this dilemma was the traditional British and American belief that sovereignty was an indivisible attribute of government.[19]

The question of sovereignty thus erected a roadblock to the creation of a workable national government. The solution, however, emanated from the earlier ratification of state constitutions, many of which contained protections for individual rights. Through the process of crafting state constitutions, observed John M. Murrin, "Americans had found a way to institutionalize an idea that all had heard about on many occasions but that no society had ever been able to convert into concrete and routine principles—the sovereignty of the people."[20] Sovereignty was not necessarily an attribute of government, but could reside in each and every individual. Viewed in this way, no division of sovereignty was necessary, for it remained at all times with the people, who could delegate it or not as they saw fit.[21]

---

[19]Murrin, p. 35.
[20]Ibid., p. 36.
[21]Ibid.

Raoul Berger has credited constitutional convention delegate James Wilson with having imported this concept into the framing of the new Constitution. In Berger's words,

> It was Wilson who triumphed over 'indivisibility' [of sovereignty] by a bold takeover: conceding that ultimate authority must be centered somewhere, he proceeded from the widely accepted axiom that power resided in the people; they could distribute it to their several agents as they thought best."[22]

For Wilson, this concept of individual sovereignty was seminal to the Constitution, for without it "we shall never be able to understand the principle on which this system was constructed."[23] Wilson has proven prescient, for the source of all the subsequent confusion about federalism is derived from a misunderstanding about the source of sovereignty. Madison likewise warned that debate over national versus state sovereignty missed the point entirely. "These gentlemen must here be reminded of their error," Madison declared. "They must be told that the ultimate authority . . . resides in the people alone."[24]

As Justice Joseph Story would later observe, the formation of the union, built as it was on the foundation of individual sovereignty, "was emphatically the act of the whole people of the united colonies" to establish a social contract.[25] Under such a social contract, according to Daniel Elazar, "powers can be divided and delegated by the sovereign people as they see fit, but sovereignty remains their inalienable possession."[26] In this type of system, Madison

[22]Raoul Berger, *Federalism: The Founders' Design* (Norman: University of Oklahoma Press, 1987), p. 51.

[23]Ibid., p. 52.

[24]*The Federalist* no. 46 (Madison), in *The Federalist Papers*, p. 305.

[25]Berger, *Federalism: The Founders' Design*, p. 26. Berger disagreed with Story, arguing that the Constitution was actually an act of independent, sovereign states. Berger later contradicted himself when he conceded that "for the Founders the *people* were sovereign." Ibid., p. 44 (emphasis in original). Either way, the result appears the same: the state conventions, acting as agents for their citizens, established a social contract on behalf of "We the People."

[26]Daniel J. Elazar, *Exploring Federalism* (Tuscaloosa: University of Alabama Press, 1987), pp. 108–9.

declared, the "federal and State governments are in fact but different agents and trustees of the people" and are therefore both subject to a "common superior."[27]

Under the proposed Constitution, the people delegated sharply circumscribed powers to the national government, such as the powers to regulate commerce and to declare war. As Felix Morley has noted, "The men who wrote the Constitution were personally familiar with the evil potential of social, religious and political monopoly," and therefore insisted on "specific safeguards" to protect against such abuses.[28] In many respects, Morley adds, the system they established "sets up roadblocks calculated to frustrate the will of the majority."[29] Among the mechanisms designed to guard against the concentration of government power were the separation of powers among the three branches of national government and the assurance of state representation in the national government through the election of senators by state legislatures.

Madison viewed the courts and the state legislatures as the two most important protectors of individual rights. The courts, Madison declared, would serve as "the guardians of those rights; they will be an impenetrable bulwark against every assumption of power in the legislature or executive; [and] they will be naturally led to resist every encroachment upon rights expressly stipulated for in the constitution by the declaration of rights."[30] Likewise, Madison predicted, "the State Legislatures will jealously and closely watch the operations of this Government, and be able to resist with more effect every assumption of power."[31]

But as Madison argued at the Constitutional Convention, the "general government" must possess sufficient affirmative powers to protect "the rights of the minority," which are placed at risk "in all cases where a majority are united by a common interest or passion."[32] Accordingly, the national government was given power to protect against violations of individual liberty by the states. For

---

[27]*The Federalist* no. 46 (Madison), pp. 304–5.

[28]Morley, p. 11.

[29]Ibid., p. 18.

[30]Madison, "Speech to the House," p. 61.

[31]Ibid.

[32]Morley, p. 27.

instance, as Robert Bork has observed, "one of the major reasons for holding the Philadelphia Convention was the states' interference with national trade. Congress was given the power to regulate interstate commerce precisely to eliminate this interference."[33] The commerce clause, argues Stephen Macedo, "reflects an original judgment that nationalizing the governance of commerce would help protect property and economic liberties from the factions and oppressive tendencies of state legislatures."[34] The authority of the national government to exercise such power to control parochial state interests was further assured by the supremacy clause of Article VI, which established the Constitution as the supreme law of the land.

Meanwhile, the original Constitution implicitly reserved to the states all legitimate powers of government that were not explicitly delegated to the national government.[35] Article IV of the Constitution guaranteed to each state a republican form of government. As Morley has observed, "Republican, as contrasted with monarchical or democratic, meant to the founding fathers the division, as opposed to the concentration, of governmental power."[36] That left the states as regulators of ordinary concerns, but it also generally entrusted them with the primary protection of individual liberty. As Hamilton explained, the state governments were charged with the task of "regulating all those personal interests and familiar concerns to which the sensibility of individuals is more immediately awake," but also were intended to serve as "the immediate and visible guardian of life and property."[37] Thomas Jefferson likewise remarked that states would provide the "most competent administrations" of day-to-day government concerns and also "the surest bulwarks against antirepublican tendencies."[38]

---

[33]Robert H. Bork, *Federalism and Federal Regulation: The Case of Product Labeling* (Washington: Washington Legal Foundation, 1991) p. 4.

[34]Stephen Macedo, *The New Right v. the Constitution* (Washington: Cato Institute, 1987), p. 62.

[35]See, for example, Berger, *Federalism: The Founders' Design*, pp. 59–61.

[36]Morley, p. 6.

[37]*The Federalist* no. 17 (Hamilton), in *The Federalist Papers*, p. 103.

[38]Quoted in Executive Order 12612 sec. 2(e), (October 26, 1987).

The discretion vested in the state governments was not absolute, however, in that the Constitution established several express limitations on state power. Article IV, for instance, established that the "Citizens of each State shall be entitled to all Privileges and Immunities of Citizens in the several States." Article 1, section 10, created additional limitations. As Madison described them, "Bills of attainder, *ex-post-facto* laws, and laws impairing the obligation of contracts, are contrary to the first principles of the social compact."[39] Their express prohibition in the Constitution, he declared, provides a "constitutional bulwark in favor of personal security and private rights."[40]

The dual allocation of powers to the national and state governments provided the principal protection for individual liberty in the original Constitution. As Alexander Hamilton argued in the New York State ratifying convention, "This balance between the national and State governments . . . is of the utmost importance. It forms a double security for the people."[41] Hamilton's argument was developed more fully in *The Federalist* no. 51, in which a case was made for a "compound" republican government with authority vested in both national and state governments:

> In a single republic, all the power surrendered by the people is submitted to the administration of a single government; and usurpations are guarded against by a division of the government into distinct and separate departments. In the compound government of America, the power surrendered by the people is first divided between two distinct governments, and then the portion allotted to each subdivided among distinct and separate departments. Hence a double security arises to the rights of the people. The different governments will control each other, at the same time that each will be controlled by itself.[42]

As Madison summarized the balance of powers between state and national governments, both would have the ability "to resist and frustrate the measures of each other."[43] The result, as Morley has

[39]*The Federalist* no. 44 (Madison), in *The Federalist Papers*, p. 291.
[40]Ibid.
[41]Quoted in Berger, *Federalism: The Founders' Design*, p. 63.
[42]*The Federalist* no. 51 (Hamilton or Madison), in *The Federalist Papers*, pp. 338–39.
[43]*The Federalist* no. 46 (Madison), p. 306.

noted, was a "balanced political structure" that was "hostile to monopolization of power, by any group, in any form."[44]

In sum, then, the original Constitution envisioned an intricate three-part structure of government: (1) sovereignty vested in the people, who delegated powers as they saw fit; (2) an explicit delegation of limited powers to the national government, including certain powers that could be exercised to restrain invasions of liberty by state governments; and (3) an implicit reservation of all remaining government powers to the states as delegated by the people, with certain explicit constitutional limitations on state power.

This structure created the basic framework of federalism that has remained essentially intact since 1787—except that protections for individual sovereignty have been significantly expanded, in the form of positive guarantees of individual rights and restraints on the power of government, first in the Bill of Rights and later in the Fourteenth Amendment.

This caveat is an important one. As we have seen—and as Madison made clear in *The Federalist*—any argument that the Framers intended to elevate either the national or the state governments at the expense of the other, or to grant plenary majoritarian powers to either or both, is flatly contradicted by the structure and history of the original Constitution. But such arguments are even more soundly repudiated by the subsequent modifications of constitutional federalism, all of which were made to further restrict the powers of government and to protect individual liberty.

Federalism and the Bill of Rights

The first expansion of constitutional protection for individual liberty was not long in coming. Indeed, concerns about potential threats to individual liberty dominated the arguments of the anti-federalists during the ratification process of the Constitution. Many feared a powerful national government that would overwhelm state constitutional protections of natural rights. George Mason warned that "the laws of the general government being paramount to the laws and constitutions of the several States, the declarations of rights in the separate States are no security."[45]

[44]Morley, pp. 31, 27.
[45]Quoted in Logan, p. 467.

Although supporters of the proposed Constitution attempted to downplay such fears, agitation for additional protections for individual rights was so intense that ratification of the Constitution was ultimately secured—and then by the slightest of margins—only upon the promise of a separate bill of rights.[46] Madison initially opposed a bill of rights because he believed that an enumeration of specific rights could be taken as disparaging unenumerated rights, but he was eventually persuaded that such modifications were necessary to secure individual rights against abuses of government power.

According to Murrin, "Madison's bill of rights protected personal liberties, not states' rights."[47] Elazar has suggested that the Framers focused on individuals rather than states "because of the growing common perception that Americans were Americans, first and foremost."[48] Explains Elazar,

> Had the states been perceived by a majority of their citizens to be primary organic communities . . ., there is little doubt that the Constitution of 1787 would have been rejected on behalf of state liberties. As it was, the real challenge to that document revolved around the protection of individual liberty (i.e. the need for a bill of rights in the federal Constitution). Not that the principle of state liberties was totally rejected—the political liberties of the states were deemed to be very important, as witness the Tenth Amendment—but they were not primary in the American scheme of things.[49]

This burgeoning national identity coincided with the generally accepted view that all Americans shared fundamental rights—rights that were derived not from citizenship in a state or in a republic, but from nature. Thus, the rights protected belonged inherently to all individuals, and the Bill of Rights protected them against interference by the government.

The first eight amendments identified specific rights and explicitly restrained the power of government to invade those rights.

[46]See, for example, Murrin, p. 40.

[47]Ibid., p. 41.

[48]Daniel J. Elazar, "Mason Versus Madison: Developing an American Theory of Federal Democracy," in Cohen, p. 75.

[49]Ibid.

Conversely, the Ninth and Tenth Amendments, respectively, affirmed that individuals possess additional rights and established a preference for decentralized authority.[50] The Ninth Amendment, in particular, was intended to preclude a narrow interpretation of the Bill of Rights that would accord protection only to those rights specifically enumerated. As James Wilson exclaimed, "Enumerate all the rights of men! I am sure, sirs, that no gentleman in the late Convention would have attempted such a thing!"[51] Randy Barnett has explained that "only a handful of the many rights proposed by state ratification conventions were eventually incorporated in the Bill of Rights. The Ninth Amendment was offered precisely to 'compensate' . . . critics for the absence of an extended list of rights."[52]

The emphasis of the Bill of Rights on individual liberty—and the reservation of certain powers to state governments within that framework—demonstrates plainly the Framers' principal concern with protecting liberty and their belief that preserving the powers of state governments provided a means to achieve that objective.

States' rights conservatives do not read the Bill of Rights that way. Raoul Berger, for instance, views the Tenth Amendment expansively, but contends that the Ninth Amendment lacks any substantive content whatsoever. "In 'retaining' the unenumerated rights," Berger argues, "the people reserved to themselves the power to add to or subtract from the rights enumerated in the Constitution by the process of amendment."[53] In other words, all the Ninth Amendment does is give people the power to amend the Constitution—a power Berger goes on to note is already "exclusively confided to them by article V."[54] Berger's theory of constitutional redundancy lacks support either in the amendment's plain language or in the motivation for its adoption.

[50]The Ninth Amendment provides: "The enumeration in the Constitution, of certain rights, shall not be construed to deny or disparage others retained by the People."

The Tenth Amendment provides: "The powers not delegated to the United States by the Constitution, nor prohibited by it to the States, are reserved to the States respectively, or to the people."

[51]Quoted in Barnett, ed., *The Rights Retained by the People*, p. 40.

[52]Ibid., p. 34.

[53]Raoul Berger, "The Ninth Amendment," in Barnett, ed., *The Rights Retained by the People*, p. 205.

[54]Ibid.

Robert Bork also thinks the Ninth Amendment is mere surplus-age, but in his construct it is redundant of the Tenth Amendment. According to Bork, "The ninth amendment appears to serve a paral-lel function [to the Tenth Amendment] by guaranteeing that the rights of the people specified already in the state constitutions were not cast in doubt by the fact that only a limited set of rights was guaranteed by the federal charter."[55] In Bork's view, the unenumer-ated rights of individuals consist only of those conferred by the state.

Bork's view is flatly at odds with the Framers' intent. "It is impos-sible to believe that human rights and individual liberties were wrung from tyrants and despots . . . only to be surrendered up to State governments where they could be destroyed by the sovereign people acting en masse," declares Bennett Patterson.[56] Of course, that is not what the Framers had in mind. To the contrary, state autonomy was viewed as a means to an end. As Hamilton viewed it, the states would provide a "complete counterpoise" to "the power of the Union."[57] Morley has observed that

> behind the determination to keep the rights of the several States inviolate was the even deeper determination to pro-tect the citizens of these states from centralized governmen-tal oppression. That is why the Republic was established not only as a federation of semi-sovereign States, but also as one of balanced authority, in which it would be extremely difficult to establish a nationwide monopoly power of any kind.[58]

In reality, the Ninth and Tenth Amendments are not redundant, and it is not at all necessary to deprive one of content so as to give meaning to the other. Both address similar concerns from different angles. As Barnett has explained, "The danger of interpreting fed-eral powers too expansively was handled by the Tenth Amend-ment, while the danger of jeopardizing unenumerated rights was

---

[55]Robert H. Bork, *The Tempting of America* (New York: Free Press, 1990), p. 185.

[56]Bennett B. Patterson, "The Forgotten Ninth Amendment," in Barnett, ed., *The Rights Retained by the People*, p. 114.

[57]*The Federalist* no. 17 (Hamilton), p. 103.

[58]Morley, p. 10.

addressed by the Ninth Amendment."[59] The Ninth Amendment established an additional protection for rights against government power, while the Tenth Amendment restricted government powers to those explicitly conferred.

Such an understanding is consistent not only with the language of the text but with the Framers' intent. As Barnett has noted, "The freedom to act within the boundaries provided by one's common law rights may be viewed as a central background presumption of the Constitution—a presumption that is reflected in the Ninth Amendment."[60] These provisions in the Bill of Rights, Barnett argues, "can be viewed as establishing a general constitutional presumption in favor of individual liberty."[61] Likewise, the Tenth Amendment by its terms creates a constitutional presumption in favor of decentralized authority, with the ultimate power reserved to the people.

The Ninth and Tenth Amendments therefore are neither inconsistent nor redundant, but are simply two different mechanisms to achieve the same goal: liberty. As such, they are essential elements in the overall construct of the Bill of Rights.

The enactment of the Bill of Rights, and particularly the Ninth and Tenth Amendments, completed the framework for federalism that would endure for most of the next century. Through the intricate constitutional mechanisms designed both to expand necessary government power while preventing tyranny, the Framers hoped to create a system that would achieve each of their initial goals: a national government strong enough to govern, retention of substantial autonomy in the states, and durable safeguards for individual rights.

The resulting product reflected a hierarchy of values that assigned the highest priority to individual liberty. The Framers' Constitution established a national government of substantial yet sharply defined powers, based on the reluctant recognition that central authority was necessary for effective government and also for the protection of liberty. It also retained broad authority in the states, grounded in the firm expectation that the states would wield their

[59]Barnett, p. 13.
[60]Ibid., p. 41.
[61]Ibid.

power in ways consistent with individual liberty. It recognized above all that the source of all government authority is the people, and that the fundamental purpose of government is to protect the sovereignty of individuals. The Framers created various mechanisms to ensure that the government they were creating would not threaten individual liberty, including negative restraints on government (such as the balance of powers between the national and state governments), as well as positive guarantees of individual rights.

The system of federalism the Framers designed was intended to create an effective government while protecting the cherished liberty that properly is the very object of government. Although tarnished over the years—perhaps beyond recognition—the system of federalism was brilliantly devised and stands as one of the Framers' most important legacies.

3. The Fourteenth Amendment: Perfecting the Design

In federalism, the Framers of the Constitution created a political masterpiece. It won assent from each of the state conventions, even though the states had to surrender a portion of their powers to the national government. It established for the first time a national government capable of governing. It formalized a national identity without sacrificing the principles of liberty on which that identity was based.

Yet it all rested upon untested hypotheses grounded in a precarious balance of powers. Would it work?

The system of federalism devised by the Framers consisted of three elements: (1) a federal government of substantial yet carefully limited powers, including the power to safeguard certain rights against violations by state governments; (2) the retention by the states of all other legitimate government powers, including the power to protect individual rights in state constitutions; and (3) sovereignty vested in the people, with explicit protections of individual rights. Whether this system would ultimately protect individual liberty in turn depended upon three premises: (1) that the balance of powers between the national and state governments would result in limitations on the powers of both; (2) that state governments would use their powers in ways consistent with individual liberty; and (3) that the protections of individual rights in the Bill of Rights would adequately secure those rights.

In practice, none of these premises proved fully correct. As myriad other studies have demonstrated, the federal government has far exceeded the constitutional limitations placed on its power; and particularly in recent years, state governments have not provided an effective bulwark against the excesses of national government power.[1] Likewise, protections of individual liberty in the Bill of

---

[1] See, for example, Felix Morley, *Freedom and Federalism* (1959; Indianapolis: Liberty Press, 1981); and Robert Higgs, *Crisis and Leviathan* (New York: Oxford University Press, 1987).

Rights and elsewhere in the Constitution have not always proven effective deterrents against violations of those rights (as the following chapters on grassroots tyranny amply illustrate).

Yet, it was the failure of the second premise—the belief that state governments would continue to safeguard individual liberty following ratification of the Constitution—that led to cataclysmic conflict during the nation's first century and thereupon led to the most important changes in our constitutional system since the Bill of Rights.

The original constitutional construct created a system of dual federalism, or what some commentators have termed dual sovereignty.[2] Under this construct, neither the national nor state governments had plenary power over the other, but rather were primary within their specific spheres of assigned authority. This system assigned two important duties to the states: day-to-day governance of ordinary affairs, and protection of individual rights. The Framers believed the states were ideally suited to the first task owing to their proximity to the people, and to the second task by virtue of their traditional role as guardians of individual liberty. The states, after all, had resisted tyrannical encroachments of the British monarchy during the colonial period, and their constitutions contained guarantees of individual rights. Their laws generally paralleled the common law, which in turn incorporated the natural rights of individuals. In this "classical" construct, the concept of states' rights was synonymous with the principles of natural rights and with the goal of the "dispersal of all power" that formed the foundation of federalism.[3]

Understandably, the Framers believed that the states would continue to vigorously and consistently protect common-law natural rights, and in the years following ratification, "the states were regarded as the prime protectors of an individual's rights and liberties."[4] Unfortunately, the state governments did not always fulfill

[2]David A. Logan, "Judicial Federalism in the Court of History" *Oregon Law Review* 66 (1988): 453, 478.

[3]Robert J. Harris, "States' Rights and Vested Interests," in *Taking the Constitution Seriously*, ed. Gary L. McDowell (Dubuque, Iowa: Kendall/Hunt Publishing Co., 1981), p. 178. Although his views are not separately discussed in chapter 1, McDowell is one of the nation's foremost scholars of federalism and one of the ablest proponents of the modern concept of states' rights federalism.

[4]Logan, p. 492.

this intended role, and over time they grew increasingly oppressive and eventually threatened the very liberty they were entrusted to protect.

The metamorphosis of state governments from guardians to violators of liberty was facilitated by the Supreme Court's decision in *Barron* v. *Mayor and City Council of Baltimore* in 1833. The case involved an action for a taking of property under the Fifth Amendment that resulted from the city's actions that caused the destruction of the value of a wharf. The Bill of Rights, ruled Justice John Marshall, provided "security against the apprehended encroachments of the general government—not against those of local governments."[5] Individuals must look to state constitutions, Marshall declared, to find limitations on the powers of state governments.[6] Making the same arguments as modern-day states' rights conservatives, Marshall argued that violations of individual rights were tolerable under the national constitution as long as they were inflicted by local governments.

The Court's decision in *Barron* was a setback for natural rights, *authorized* by the very Court that often invoked such rights as a basis for its decisions, leaving "the states free to nullify basic rights, including the right to property,"[7] as Michael Kent Curtis has charged. As with many Supreme Court decisions, the specific questions before the Court in *Barron* were a surrogate for more important and divisive issues that the Court was hesitant to confront directly. Against the backdrop of the burgeoning debate over slavery, *Barron* provided the Court with an opportunity to placate southern states by crafting a judicial rationale for states' rights. As a result, Curtis concludes, the *Barron* decision "promoted the stability of the Union at the expense of liberty" by allowing southern states to "deny procedural and substantive rights to blacks."[8]

Indeed, the *Barron* decision came just as the issue of sovereignty, which the Framers had attempted to resolve through the system of federalism, was reemerging as a major subject of national debate.

---

[5]32 U.S. 243, 250 (1833).

[6]Ibid. at 247–48.

[7]Michael Kent Curtis, *No State Shall Abridge* (Durham, N.C.: Duke University Press, 1986), p. 23.

[8]Ibid.

As Daniel Elazar has explained, "The federal principle represent[ed] an alternative to (and a radical attack upon) the modern idea of sovereignty," in that it establishes sovereignty in the people rather than in any particular body of government.[9] As a consequence, one of federalism's major attributes was its "reduction of the question of political sovereignty to an incidental one,"[10] for in matters affecting the rights of the people, neither national nor state governments are sovereign.

But the defenders of slavery had other ideas, and they sought to exhume the concept of state sovereignty. The leading architect of this movement was John C. Calhoun, who argued that the states rather than the nation were the "primary organic communities,"[11] thereby establishing state rather than national citizenship as the source of an individual's political identity. In the process, Calhoun completely reversed the Framers' understanding of states' rights as a means of protecting individual liberty. Instead, he

> denied generally the doctrine of natural rights in its traditional context, and converted the principle of states' rights into an instrumentality . . ., with the protection of slavery foremost in his consideration. In so doing he extracted from states' rights principles most of the vestiges of revolutionary and natural rights philosophy.[12]

During the 1830s, Calhoun and the other states' rights advocates rallied behind the banner of "nullification," the doctrine that states could refuse to obey enactments of the national government to which they objected.[13] The question of nullification arose when southern states objected to federally enacted tariffs, which were designed to protect northern manufacturing products against foreign competition. In this instance, the states were performing the role assigned to them under the federalist system—namely, protecting individual liberty (the right of free trade) against interference by the national government. The objections to the tariffs were cast

[9]Daniel J. Elazar, *Exploring Federalism* (Tuscaloosa: University of Alabama Press, 1987), pp. 108–9.

[10]Ibid.

[11]Ibid., p. 94.

[12]Harris, p. 179.

[13]Logan, pp. 475–76.

not in terms of liberty, however, but in terms of state sovereignty. In 1832, South Carolina declared federal import tariffs null and void and threatened to withdraw from the union if the laws were enforced. President Andrew Jackson countered that secession was unconstitutional. The "nullification crisis" was averted by congressional compromise,[14] but the doctrine of state sovereignty continued to build momentum as southern states chafed under a national government dominated by northerners.

State sovereignty also provided a convenient rationale for the perpetuation of slavery, particularly as a basis for resisting efforts of the national government to abolish it. The abdication by the federal judiciary of its primary role in protecting individual liberty— a process that commenced with the *Barron* decision and culminated in the Supreme Court's adoption of the states' rights philosophy in the infamous *Dred Scott* decision[15]—"left the states free to nullify basic rights."[16] As David Logan has recounted, the states' rights philosophy operated as an effective restraint against "national interference with the slave owners' economic and social system," in which state property laws were invoked to ensure control over human possessions.[17]

Meanwhile, southern legislatures aggressively enacted laws restricting freedom of speech and press in an effort to suppress antislavery ideas. States also passed laws requiring local postmasters to inspect mail so as to censor abolitionist propaganda, and local governments refused to provide ordinary protections to abolitionists against mob violence.[18]

But as states' rights advocates grew bolder in their oppression, they were unwittingly sowing the seeds of their own demise. Those

[14]Ibid., p. 476 n. 110.

[15]*Dred Scott* v. *Sandford*, 60 U.S. 663 (1857). As Robert J. Harris observed, the Supreme Court under Chief Justice Roger Taney accorded "juristic recognition" to John C. Calhoun's concept of states' rights and repudiation of natural rights principles. Harris, p. 179. In *Dred Scott*, the Court ruled against an emancipated slave who sought standing to sue in the courts, holding that blacks were entitled only to such rights as "the government might choose to grant them." For a discussion of *Dred Scott* and its broader implications, see Clint Bolick, *Changing Course: Civil Rights at the Crossroads* (New Brunswick, N.J.: Transaction Books, 1988), pp. 21–22.

[16]Curtis, p. 23.

[17]Logan, pp. 477–78.

[18]Curtis, pp. 30–31. See also Bolick, *Changing Course*, pp. 19–21.

who remained faithful to natural rights principles began to question the premise, which was essential to the original system of federalism, that state governments were reliable guardians of individual liberty. On the contrary, Madison's warnings a half-century earlier about the propensity for tyranny to take root in more localized governments were proving increasingly prophetic. "The antislavery champions," according to Harold M. Hyman, "perceived correctly that injustices were overwhelmingly local and state, that federal justice had been irrelevant as a remedy, and that dual federalism failed" in its mission of protecting liberty.[19] The struggle over slavery convinced northerners that "it was the states, and not the federal government, that presented the greatest threat to individual liberties."[20]

These arguments provided the ideological backdrop for the Civil War. Even though President Abraham Lincoln persistently violated civil liberties during the war in the name of preserving the Union, the struggle against slavery provided an important moral justification for the northerners. Conversely, the entire notion of the Confederacy exemplified the concept of state sovereignty and of the states as the primary organic communities. By withdrawing from the Union, the South repudiated a constitutional system dedicated to individual liberty and instead embraced an ideology that glorified state over individual rights. The war was, in this important sense, a battle for sovereignty between individuals and states.[21]

These ideological battles continued in the aftermath of the Civil War, and the emergent radical Republican majority in Congress dedicated itself to curing the constitutional deficiencies that had allowed states to run roughshod over individual liberties. Ultimately, as J. M. Balkin has commented, the "new way of thinking" about states as violators rather than guardians of individual liberty

[19]Harold M. Hyman, "Federalism: Legal Fiction and Historical Artifact?" *Brigham Young University Law Review* 15 (1987): 905, 919.

[20]J. M. Balkin, "Federalism and the Conservative Ideology," *Urban Lawyer* 19 (1987): 473.

[21]The North, of course, was hardly pristine in its support for individual liberty. The imposition of oppressive tariffs, the creation of a military draft, and the suspension of habeas corpus were among the instances of tyranny supported by the northern states and effectuated by the national government. What I am focusing on here are the terms of the debate over which the war was fought, which in turn influenced the enactments of the Reconstruction Congress.

"was embodied in the language of the Fourteenth Amendment, which, along with the other Civil War amendments, drastically altered the balance of power between the states and the federal government."[22]

The Reconstruction Congress was unlike any other, before or since. More than at any time since the American Revolution, Congress concerned itself with questions of principle and sought to implement a clear and cohesive natural rights vision. Emboldened by their triumph in a war they perceived as a battle over competing moral visions—and lacking effective congressional opposition—the radical Republicans were able to make fundamental changes in the basic law of the land in conformity with their vision.[23]

Central to their vision was the need to establish effective deterrents against the power of state governments to violate individual natural rights. Michael Kent Curtis has stated that "perhaps the most common Republican refrain in the [Reconstruction] Congress was that life, liberty, and property of American citizens must be protected against denial by the states."[24]

Opposition to these efforts was based, not surprisingly, on states' rights grounds.[25] But, as Curtis observes,

> arguments by Democrats that the protection of fundamental rights would interfere with the legitimate rights of states struck Republicans as absurd. No state retained the legitimate authority to deprive citizens of their fundamental rights because government, at all levels, was designed to protect such rights.[26]

Nonetheless, the Republicans were not out to destroy the states, but merely to provide stronger safeguards against violations of individual rights by state governments. Curtis continues:

> Although Republicans rejected the notion that states could invade the fundamental rights of citizens, they still

[22]Ibid.

[23]For a comprehensive discussion of the history and purposes of the Fourteenth Amendment, see Clint Bolick, *Unfinished Business: A Civil Rights Strategy for America's Third Century* (San Francisco: Pacific Research Institute, 1990). The book presents a strategy to effectuate the purposes of the Fourteenth Amendment.

[24]Curtis, p. 41.

[25]Logan, pp. 500–501.

[26]Curtis, p. 41.

wanted to preserve the states. They did not want the federal government to supplant them altogether or usurp their basic functions. . . . But although Republicans wanted to preserve the states, they did not sympathize with the doctrine of states' rights advanced by slaveholders and their Democratic allies in Congress in the years before the Civil War—a doctrine that permitted some citizens to deny the rights of others.[27]

As with the original Constitution and Bill of Rights, the advocates of liberty achieved their objectives by establishing new protections for individual rights and additional restraints on government power—this time, limits specifically applicable to state governments. To enforce these rights and restraints required an expansion of federal government power, but only as far as necessary to protect individual liberty. Indeed, the most significant development during this period was the transfer of primary authority for the protection of rights from the states to the national government. As Logan has noted, the various enactments in the post–Civil War era "dramatically expanded the jurisdiction of the federal courts by authorizing them to enforce new individual rights."[28]

The resolve of Congress was strengthened by the adoption of "black codes" by southern legislatures between 1865 and 1867. These codes were designed to ensure that blacks would remain economically subservient by denying them such rights as freedom of contract, the right to own and exchange private property, and protection of the laws for personal security.[29] As Sen. Henry Wilson remarked, federal legislation was necessary to counteract "atrocious" laws that are "wholly incompatible with the freedom of these freedmen"—laws that were "persistently carried into effect by the local authorities."[30] Sen. Charles Sumner, the leader of the

[27]Ibid.

[28]Logan, p. 458. I quarrel a bit with Logan's wording here; the rights protected by the post–Civil War era enactments were all natural rights and hence were not "new individual rights." What was new was the clear authority of the national government to protect them against violations by state governments.

[29]See, for example, Bolick, *Changing Course*, p. 25.

[30]See Alfred Avins, ed., *The Reconstruction Amendments' Debates* (Wilmington: Delaware Law School, 1974), p. 138. This statement was made in support of the Civil Rights Act of 1866, as were those in the notes immediately following.

radical Republicans, rejected the states' rights objections to federal civil rights legislation. Declared Sumner, "From the beginning State Rights have been used for oppression and wrong. The terrible war from which we are emerging," which was "a rebellion in the name of State Rights, . . . makes it an especial duty now to restrain them, not to extend them."[31]

The first step in fulfilling this vision was the Civil Rights Act of 1866, which established federal protection for basic natural rights, "any law . . . to the contrary notwithstanding." As Sen. Lyman Trumbull summarized its basic provisions, the civil rights bill "declares that all persons in the United States shall be entitled to the same civil rights, the right to the fruit of their own labor, the right to make contracts, the right to buy and sell, and enjoy liberty and happiness."[32]

Some critics, including President Andrew Johnson, questioned the constitutionality of the new law, leading its proponents to "constitutionalize" the provisions of the civil rights act in the Fourteenth Amendment. Ratified in 1868, the Fourteenth Amendment provides that

> no State shall make or enforce any law which shall abridge
> the privileges or immunities of citizens of the United States;
> nor shall any State deprive any person of life, liberty, or
> property, without due process of law; nor deny to any per-
> son within its jurisdiction the equal protection of the laws.

The amendment also delegated to Congress the authority to enforce its provisions through appropriate legislation.

Each of the protections provided by the Fourteenth Amendment was rooted in the natural law philosophy of the Framers of the Constitution. The due process clause established safeguards that limited the power of states to deprive individuals of life, liberty, and property, and the privileges or immunities clause and the equal protection clause placed absolute limits on the exercise of state power. The privileges or immunities clause recognized a spectrum of individual liberties (the rights enumerated in the Bill of Rights

[31]Ibid., p. 172.
[32]Ibid., p. 136.

as well as the unenumerated rights protected by the Ninth Amendment) that the states henceforth would have no power to violate.[33] Likewise, the equal protection clause, heeding Madison's warnings about the power of "factions" to manipulate political power to benefit some and burden others, created a prohibition against arbitrary and unequal legislation.[34]

Once the Fourteenth Amendment was ratified, Congress took further steps to enforce its guarantees. "The principal danger that menaces us to-day," declared Rep. George F. Hoar, "is from the effort within the States to deprive considerable numbers of persons of the civil and equal rights which the General Government is endeavoring to secure to them."[35] As a result, Congress passed the Civil Rights Act of 1871, which among other provisions created a private cause of action in federal courts for deprivations of federally protected rights committed "under color of State law," as well as criminal sanctions against those who conspired to violate such rights. In response to arguments that state courts should provide the principal recourse for such deprivations, Sen. Oliver P. Morton declared,

> It is said that these crimes should be punished by the States; that they are already offenses against the laws of the States, and the matter should be left with the States. The answer to that is, that the States do not punish them; the States do not protect the rights of the people; the State courts are powerless to redress these wrongs. The great fact remains that large classes of people . . . are without legal remedy in the courts of the States. Should this fact be overlooked for the sake of a theory?[36]

It is fair to say that the concept of states' rights was not warmly embraced by the framers of the Fourteenth Amendment. On the contrary, they understood that they were effecting a "fundamental

---

[33]For a discussion of the purposes and subsequent evisceration of the privileges or immunities clause, see Bolick, *Unfinished Business*, pp. 47–91.

[34]Ibid., pp. 93–133.

[35]Quoted in Logan, p. 509. These quotations are from the debates over the Civil Rights Act of 1871.

[36]Ibid.

change in the federal relationship"[37]: a substantial expansion of the power of the national government, for the sole purpose of protecting individual liberty against the oppressions of state governments.

Modern-day proponents of states' rights minimize the significance of the Fourteenth Amendment. Raoul Berger, for instance, claimed that the amendment's framers "confined it to protection of carefully enumerated rights against State discrimination, deliberately withholding federal power to supply those rights where they were not granted by a State to anybody, white or black."[38] Although that was a "tragically limited" response to the problems of the day, lamented Berger, "it was all the sovereign people were prepared to do in 1868."[39]

This narrow interpretation of the amendment deprives it of its essential meaning. Berger treated the privileges or immunities clause, as he did the Ninth Amendment, as if it were written in disappearing ink. Once again the framers of a constitutional provision did not mean what they said. In Berger's constitutional universe, the protection of privileges or immunities, like the protection of unenumerated rights in the Ninth Amendment, amounted to nothing.[40]

To the contrary, the Reconstruction Congress understood, as expressed by Rep. William Lawrence, that the new national protections of individual rights were "scarcely less to the people of this country than the Magna Charta was to the people of England."[41] As Edward Erler has observed, "It was well understood by the thirty-ninth Congress that the purpose of the Fourteenth Amendment was to extend the protection of individual rights to all people"[42]—in essence, incorporating into the basic law of the land "the

[37]Edward J. Erler, "The Fourteenth Amendment and the Protection of Minority Rights," *Brigham Young University Law Review* (1987): 977, 981.

[38]Raoul Berger, *Government by Judiciary* (Cambridge, Mass.: Harvard University Press, 1977), p. 407.

[39]Ibid.

[40]The substantive content of privileges or immunities is fairly readily discerned from both the legislative history and from the catalogue of rights protected in the Bill of Rights and in the Civil Rights Act of 1866, which virtually all scholars agree the Fourteenth Amendment was intended to constitutionalize. These catalogued rights included economic liberty, freedom of contract, ownership and exchange of property, and personal security. See generally Bolick, *Unfinished Business*, pp. 47–91.

[41]Quoted in Ibid., p. 26.

[42]Erler, p. 1001.

natural rights principles set forth in the Declaration of Independence."[43] The amendment's framers made certain that these rights would be enforced, explains Stephen Macedo, by "decisively shift-[ing] to the national government the responsibility for protecting a broad sphere of individual rights against the states."[44]

The Fourteenth Amendment substantially altered the relationship and the balance of powers between the national government and the states. Whereas the constitutional system of federalism prior to the Fourteenth Amendment assigned to the states the primary role of protecting fundamental rights, that role was now reassigned to the national government. The greatest power shift accrued in the federal judiciary, which now was entrusted with the protection of rights against both federal and state deprivations.

Of course, the Fourteenth Amendment did not supplant the Tenth Amendment. The states were still free to exercise such legitimate government powers as were not expressly delegated to the national government; likewise, they were intended to remain as effective deterrents against excesses of the national government, particularly in enforcing their own protections of individual liberty. The national government was given substantial new power, but only to be exercised as a negative restraint against the oppressions of the states. A powerful new check was added to the existing constitutional system of checks and balances to safeguard individual liberty.

With the ratification of the Fourteenth Amendment, the constitutional design of federalism was complete. This design expanded and improved upon existing constitutional provisions, most notably the reservation of individual rights embodied in the Ninth Amendment, and the preference for decentralized authority established in the Tenth Amendment. This hierarchy of constitutional values, in which individual liberty and decentralized authority are paramount, is reflected in the following constitutional delineation of rights and powers:

INDIVIDUAL LIBERTY
Sovereignty resides with individuals, who may delegate certain powers to government; but they retain their natural rights, which are inalienable.

[43]Ibid., p. 981.

[44]Stephen Macedo, *The New Right v. the Constitution* (Washington: Cato Institute, 1987), p. 21.

STATE GOVERNMENTS

The states possess all legitimate governmental powers not expressly delegated to the national government, particularly the power to regulate day-to-day affairs for the general good.

NATIONAL GOVERNMENT

The federal government possesses only those powers specifically delegated to it, including the power to protect individuals against state violations of their natural rights and to ensure due process and equal protection of the laws.

This hierarchy of values and the resulting constitutional division of rights and powers in turn create constitutional presumptions in favor of individual liberty and decentralized authority. In practice, that means that conflicts among these competing values should be resolved in the following manner:

1. Conflicts between individual liberty and the power of the national government should be resolved in favor of individual liberty, unless the conflict involves an expressly delegated power, which should be exercised in a manner that infringes upon individual rights as little as possible.
2. Conflicts between individual liberty and the power of state governments should be resolved in favor of individual liberty, unless the conflict involves an exercise of legitimate state police powers exercised in a way that infringes upon individual rights as little as possible.
3. Conflicts between state governments and the national government should be resolved in favor of the states, unless the national government is acting pursuant to an expressly delegated power, including the power to protect individual liberty.

This is federalism, as the Framers of the Constitution and the framers of the Fourteenth Amendment created and understood it. This system of federalism, were it to work as it was designed, would ensure an effective government that would always respect the principal purpose of government: to secure individual rights.

Indeed, it is a tribute to the architects of American federalism that their experiment has worked so well. Despite the growth of the national government, ours remains a fairly decentralized society, with many decisions reserved to state and local governments, and with a degree of individual liberty still unknown in most of the world. And, true to the intent of the framers of the Fourteenth Amendment, the national government often has stepped in to protect individual liberty.

But the system of federalism has not always worked in accordance with its ambitious objectives. Instances of the federal government exceeding its carefully delineated powers at the expense of precious individual liberties are legion. What is often overlooked, however, is the continuing propensity of state and local governments to violate individual rights, and the failure of the federal judiciary to halt such abuses. The collapse of a system of federalism dedicated to individual liberty is the subject of the next chapter, with the resulting contemporary phenomenon of grassroots tyranny illustrated in the chapters that follow.

4. The Contemporary Quagmire

The carefully woven tapestry of federalism did not stay together for long. Thread by thread, the restraints placed upon the power of both state and federal governments were weakened, destroying bit by bit the delicate protections of individual liberty that had been painstakingly crafted by the architects of the Constitution, the Bill of Rights, and the Fourteenth Amendment. Over the course of more than a century, we have entrenched in our law today a hopelessly confused and muddled concept of federalism, a concept sapped of the vitality of its original moral underpinnings.

The primary culprit in undoing the Framers' handiwork is the Supreme Court. Starting shortly after the adoption of the Fourteenth Amendment and continuing to this day, the Court has engaged in two types of judicial activism: the kind that creates entitlements and government powers out of thin air, and the kind (often erroneously referred to as "judicial restraint") that reads out of the Constitution some of its most vital protections of individual liberty. The judiciary has allowed the power of government to expand far beyond its intended limits, abdicating in many instances its central role in protecting individuals against abuses of government power. The effect of the Court's jurisprudence during the past century is to nullify the constitutional doctrine of federalism and many of the vital liberties it was designed to protect.

Other forces also contributed to the decline of federalism, including the expansion of national power, the growth of state and local governments, and the reemergence of the doctrine of states' rights among those who purport to defend federalism. In combination, these factors fundamentally altered the concept of federalism by weakening its structural supports and by divorcing it from its underlying values. As a result, our system of government today is precisely the opposite of what the Framers intended, with government—particularly at the national level but also at the state and local levels—possessing most of the power in society, leaving individuals with precious little autonomy. Each of these phenomena is explored below.

The Abandonment of Liberty

The Supreme Court made quick work of the Fourteenth Amendment and its vital restraints against abuses of individual liberty by state governments. "From 1868 to 1925 [the Supreme Court] found very few . . . liberties protected from state action," Michael Kent Curtis has observed. "Those [liberties] the states were free to flout (so far as federal limitations were concerned) . . . include[d] free speech, press, religion, the right to jury trial, freedom from self-incrimination, from infliction of cruel and unusual punishments, and more."[1]

Eager to "preserve what they asserted were the virtues of [pre–Civil War] federalism,"[2] a majority on the Supreme Court moved aggressively to restrict the scope of the recently adopted Fourteenth Amendment, beginning with the evisceration of the amendment's most important component—the protection of the "privileges or immunities" of citizens against abridgement by state governments. "Unique among constitutional provisions," Edward Corwin remarked, "the privileges and immunities clause of the Fourteenth Amendment enjoys the distinction of having been rendered a 'practical nullity' by a single decision of the Supreme Court rendered within five years after its ratification."[3] This ruling, rendered in the 1873 *Slaughter-House Cases*,[4] is often overlooked in contemporary legal debates yet stands as one of the most sweeping and debilitating repudiations of individual liberty in the history of American jurisprudence.[5]

In *Slaughter-House*, the Supreme Court essentially nullified a constitutional amendment that was designed to broadly secure liberties. Foremost among the liberties that the framers of the Fourteenth

[1]Michael Kent Curtis, *No State Shall Abridge* (Durham, N.C.: Duke University Press, 1986), p. 1.

[2]Harold M. Hyman, "Federalism: Legal Fiction and Historical Artifact?" *Brigham Young University Law Review* 15 (1987): 905, 922.

[3]Quoted in Philip B. Kurland, "The Privileges or Immunities Clause: 'Its Hour Come Round at Last'?" *Washington University Law Quarterly* (1972): 405, 413.

[4]83 U.S. 36 (1873).

[5]See Clint Bolick, *Unfinished Business: A Civil Rights Strategy for America's Third Century* (San Francisco: Pacific Research Insitute, 1990), pp. 47–91.

Amendment sought to protect was "economic liberty"—the freedom to pursue a business or occupation free from arbitrary or excessive government interference. The infamous black codes, adopted by southern legislatures in the years immediately following the Civil War, were aimed at destroying the economic liberty of the newly emancipated blacks. By means of the coercive apparatus of state governments, the codes established a labor cartel and placed it beyond the reach of competitive free-market forces, thereby ensuring a servile labor market for the plantation owners. The black codes were a primary target of the Civil Rights Act of 1866, which was designed to counteract the codes by guaranteeing such essential rights as freedom of contract and the right to own and exchange property. These rights, along with others such as those enumerated in the Bill of Rights, constituted the "privileges or immunities" of citizenship that were subsequently protected against infringement by the states in the Fourteenth Amendment.[6]

The *Slaughter-House Cases* provided the first major test of this protection.[7] In March 1869, the Louisiana legislature granted an exclusive 25-year slaughterhouse monopoly and ordered the closing of other existing slaughterhouses. Although the law served some valid health and safety objectives, its passage was secured by massive bribery, "with its most immediate beneficiaries—the seventeen participants in the corporation it established—adroitly distributing shares of stock and cash."[8] The law was immediately challenged by a group of butchers whose livelihoods were jeopardized by the blatantly protectionist legislation as a violation of the Fourteenth Amendment's protection of the privileges or immunities of citizenship.

On April 14, 1873, the Supreme Court voted 5-4 to sustain the law in its entirety. But as Michael Kent Curtis has charged, the Court went far beyond the facts of the case, interpreting the Fourteenth Amendment's protections "so narrowly that the privileges or immunities clause was virtually read out of the Constitution."[9]

---

[6]For a superb analysis of the history and intent of the privileges or immunities clause, with particular emphasis on its protection of the liberties enumerated in the Bill of Rights, see Curtis.

[7]Ibid., pp. 54–60.

[8]Charles A. Lofgren, *The Plessy Case* (New York: Oxford University Press, 1987), p. 67.

[9]Curtis, p. 173.

Writing for the majority, Justice Samuel F. Miller conceded that the economic liberties asserted by the butchers were within the privileges or immunities of citizenship. But Miller concluded that the Fourteenth Amendment was designed to protect against the states only those rights that derived from national citizenship as defined by national law—the right of habeas corpus, the right to access to navigable waters within the United States, the right to move freely from state to state and to enjoy the same rights as citizens of those states, and so on. Conversely, the rights asserted by the butchers, according to the majority, were rights "which belong to citizens of the States as such, and . . . [are not] placed under the special care of the Federal government" by virtue of the Fourteenth Amendment.[10]

By this ruling, Miller not only negated the meaning of the privileges or immunities clause, but also repudiated the principle of individual sovereignty embodied in the Constitution. *Slaughter-House* thus embraced the notion—one that remains popular among modern states' rights conservatives—that the rights of individuals are derived not from their nature as human beings but by virtue of their state citizenship. Under this view, the Fourteenth Amendment changed little, in that individuals still were obliged to turn to state governments for protection of their most basic rights. If the states declined to provide such protections—indeed, if the states themselves were the violators—individuals had no recourse. The rights asserted, although universally recognized as fundamental, were therefore illusory in reality. The principles over which both the American Revolution and the Civil War had been fought were thus nullified by the same high court whose basic purpose under our constitutional system is to uphold those principles.

The grave implications of the majority decision in *Slaughter-House* were not lost upon the four dissenting justices. Proclaiming that "our duty is to execute the law, not make it," Justice Noah Swayne protested that the majority's unprincipled activism "defeats, by a limitation not anticipated, the intent of those by whom the instrument was framed."[11] As Justice Stephen Field viewed it, the majority had virtually repealed a vital part of the Fourteenth Amendment.

[10]*Slaughter-House Cases*, at 78.
[11]Ibid., at 129 (Swayne, J., dissenting).

If the amendment does not protect economic liberty among the privileges or immunities of citizens, Field proclaimed, "it was a vain and idle enactment, which accomplished nothing, and most unnecessarily excited Congress and the people on its passage."[12]

In reality, as Swayne recounted, the Fourteenth Amendment marked "an important epoch in the constitutional history of the country."[13] In the Constitution as it existed before the Civil War, Swayne explained, "ample protection was given against oppression by the Union, but little was given against wrong and oppression by the States."[14] The protections of individual liberty in the Fourteenth Amendment, conversely, "trench directly upon the power of the States, and deeply affect those bodies."[15] Thus understood, declared Swayne, the Civil War amendments "may be said to rise to the dignity of a new Magna Charta."[16]

Another dissenter, Justice Joseph P. Bradley, articulated a two-part inquiry that the Court should apply whenever it reviews state regulations that restrict individual liberty: whether the individual's actions are among the rights and privileges of American citizens, and whether the regulation of that activity is reasonable. Finding that the right to pursue a trade or profession "is an essential part of that liberty which it is the object of government to protect," Justice Bradley went on to conclude that the creation of a slaughter-house monopoly was not a reasonable regulation, but was instead "one of those arbitrary and unjust laws made in the interest of a few scheming individuals."[17] In the dissenters' view, then, those aspects of the law violated the privileges or immunities of American citizenship, and were therefore unconstitutional.

Field lamented the majority's decision to uphold the law, "for by it the right of free labor, one of the most sacred and imprescriptible rights of man, is violated."[18] Meanwhile, Swayne expressed the "hope that the consequences to follow may prove less serious and

[12]Ibid., at 96 (Field, J., dissenting).
[13]Ibid., at 125 (Swayne, J., dissenting).
[14]Ibid., at 129.
[15]Ibid., at 125.
[16]Ibid.
[17]Ibid., at 116, 120 (Bradley, J., dissenting).
[18]Ibid., at 110 (Field, J., dissenting).

far-reaching than the minority fear they will be."[19] But his hopes were not to be realized. Although states' rights conservatives such as Robert Bork dismiss the *Slaughter-House* decision as "a narrow victory for judicial moderation,"[20] the real-world consequences of the decision ultimately would "adversely affect the daily lives of millions of Americans."[21] For *Slaughter-House*, whose pernicious doctrine remains on the books today, unleashed state governments to enact oppressive laws without fear that the courts would strike down such laws as violations of individual liberty.[22]

White supremacists in the South promptly took advantage of this judicial abdication to enact Jim Crow laws, in which the coercive apparatus of state governments was used to severely limit economic opportunities and social integration for blacks. These laws led to another major judicial confrontation between individual liberty and states' rights over the pernicious doctrine of "separate but equal" public facilities in the infamous 1896 *Plessy* v. *Ferguson* case.[23] Again, the state of Louisiana was involved, this time mandating separate railroad cars for blacks and whites. Objecting to this interference with voluntary contractual relationships, the railroad company helped develop test cases to challenge the law.

The case that made it to the Court was that of Homer Plessy, who was one-eighth black and was imprisoned when he refused his assignment to a colored railroad car. Because the privileges or immunities clause was not available to Plessy to vindicate his economic liberty, he relied on the equal protection clause of the Fourteenth Amendment. By an 8-1 vote, however, the Supreme Court in the *Plessy* decision did to the equal protection clause what it had done to the privileges or immunities clause 23 years earlier in *Slaughter-House*, essentially reading out of the Constitution the prohibition against patently discriminatory state laws. *Plessy* thus removed another vital restraint against government power, thereby allowing states to run roughshod over individual liberty.[24]

[19]Ibid., at 130 (Swayne, J., dissenting).

[20]Robert H. Bork, *The Tempting of America* (New York: Free Press, 1990), p. 39.

[21]Hyman, p. 922.

[22]For a discussion of the real-world implications of *Slaughter-House*, see Bolick, pp. 68–76.

[23]163 U.S. 537 (1896).

[24]The "separate but equal" doctrine was repudiated by *Brown* v. *Board of Education*, 347 U.S. 483 (1954), but *Plessy* itself was never overruled, and it retains jurisprudential vitality even today. See Bolick, pp. 102–4.

72

In the years since *Slaughter-House* and *Plessy*, the Supreme Court has never fulfilled the Fourteenth Amendment's great promise. The amendment's protection of the privileges or immunities of American citizens remains completely eviscerated; the equal protection clause has achieved its enormous potential only as a restraint against state-imposed racial discrimination, and even there it is only selectively applied.[25]

Nonetheless, at different times the Court has breathed life into the Fourteenth Amendment in different ways. A conservative Court prior to the New Deal used the amendment's due process clause to shield entrepreneurial activities against arbitrary or excessive economic regulation by the states,[26] and to protect such personal liberties as the right of parents to direct and control the education of their children.[27] When liberals gained control of the Court in the 1930s, they dispensed with judicial protection of economic liberty,[28] but instead used the due process clause to "incorporate" most of the protections of the Bill of Rights into the Fourteenth Amendment.[29] Subsequently, the Court has applied against the states those Bill of Rights protections it has deemed "fundamental to the American scheme of justice," such as freedom of speech and press, free exercise of religion, freedom against self-incrimination, and freedom from unreasonable searches and seizures of persons and property.[30] In more recent years, an increasingly conservative Court has scaled back those protections somewhat, but has taken tentative steps to protect private-property rights against excessive regulation by state and local governments.[31] This record demon-

[25]See, for example, ibid., pp. 106–13. However, the Court has occasionally applied the equal protection clause to strike down oppressive and patently arbitrary laws. See, for example, *City of Cleburne* v. *Cleburne Living Center*, 473 U.S. 432 (1985).

[26]See, for example, *Lochner* v. *New York*, 198 U.S. 45 (1905).

[27]See, for example, *Pierce* v. *Society of Sisters*, 268 U.S. 510 (1925). Unlike other cases from this period, the *Pierce* line of cases remains authoritative today.

[28]See, for example, *West Coast Hotel Co.* v. *Parrish*, 300 U.S. 379 (1937).

[29]See Curtis, p. 197.

[30]Ibid., p. 203.

[31]See, for example, *Nollan* v. *California Coastal Commission*, 483 U.S. 825 (1987). In this area, the Court is applying to the states the Fifth Amendment's prohibition against the taking of private property for public use without just compensation (the takings clause). For a compelling discussion of how the takings clause should be used to constrain government power, see Richard A. Epstein, *Takings* (Cambridge, Mass.: Harvard University Press, 1985).

strates that neither liberals nor conservatives are prepared to consistently apply the full range of restraints against government power as intended by the framers of the Fourteenth Amendment.

Meanwhile, the Court's attitude toward federalism has swung back and forth in pendulum-like fashion. When the conservatives were using the due process clause to strike down state economic regulations, the liberals were advocates of states' rights. When the liberals have applied the Bill of Rights and Fourteenth Amendment to strike down state and local laws favored by the conservatives, the conservatives have assumed the states' rights mantle.

But it was the dramatic expansion of national power during the 1930s that firmly established liberals as enemies and conservatives as defenders of states' rights federalism. As of 1927, government in America remained largely decentralized, with state and local governments performing most public functions. The national government was eclipsed in size and scope by state and local governments, which had twice the tax revenues and four times the personnel of the national government.[32]

The primacy of state and local governments eroded rapidly during the New Deal, when the national regulatory and welfare apparatus grew at a voracious pace. This movement of government power toward Washington was accomplished in large part through a sweeping application of the interstate commerce power, which was used to justify virtually any exercise of national regulatory power.[33]

Such a major expansion of national power also required the evisceration of the Tenth Amendment, which had expressly reserved to the states all legitimate government powers not expressly delegated to the national government. The amendment was essentially repealed by the Supreme Court in a series of decisions culminating in *United States* v. *Darby* in 1941, in which the Court upheld federal minimum-wage and maximum-hours laws as a valid exercise of the national commerce power.[34] The Court concluded that the Tenth Amendment placed no restraint on such an expansion of national

---

[32]Robert B. Hawkins, Jr., "Federalism: The Contemporary Challenge," in *Federalism: The Legacy of George Mason*, ed. Martin B. Cohen (Fairfax, Va.: George Mason University Press, 1988), pp. 110–11.

[33]Ibid., p. 112. Article I, section 8, of the Constitution vests in Congress the power to "regulate Commerce . . . among the several States."

[34]312 U.S. 100 (1941).

power, declaring that "the amendment states but a truism that all is retained which has not been surrendered. There is nothing in the history of its adoption to suggest that it was more than declaratory of the relationship between the national and state governments."[35]

The doctrine embraced by the Court in *Darby*, combined with the failure of both liberals and conservatives to consistently support the full range of individual liberties, shifted the focus of concerns about federalism away from individual liberty and toward states' rights. In the years during and after the New Deal, the lines of political debate typically were drawn not in terms of government power versus individual liberty, but in terms of national versus state power. Whereas in *Darby* the state's interest happened to coincide with individual liberty—the freedom of individuals to bargain over the terms and conditions of employment—in subsequent cases those who championed states' rights often would find themselves arguing against individual liberty. In this manner, federalism—mistaken as a surrogate for states' rights—was pressed into service to oppose all manner of national initiatives, including those promoting individual liberty.

Perhaps most notable in this regard was the opposition of states' rights conservatives—under the banner of federalism—to school desegregation and the Supreme Court's 1954 *Brown* v. *Board of Education* decision.[36] To states' rights conservatives, it did not matter that these exercises of national power were intended to effectuate the Fourteenth Amendment's vital protections of individual liberty against oppression by state governments. What mattered was that the national government was challenging a previously unchallenged prerogative of state governments—in this instance, the power to discriminate.[37]

As federalism and states' rights grew ever more intertwined, federalism increasingly was perceived as a reactionary doctrine. In the process, its vitality in stemming the expansion of national power

[35] Ibid., at 124.

[36] 347 U.S. 483 (1954).

[37] For a thoughtful commentary on the unfortunate role of conservatives in civil rights issues during the 1950s and 1960s, see Charles Murray's foreword in Bolick, pp. ix-xiii.

diminished considerably. By invoking federalism in defense of such pernicious practices as state-imposed racial segregation, the apologists for such policies seriously undermined the moral foundation upon which the concept of federalism was built.

The breathtaking expansion of national power during the past six decades thus has yielded mixed results for federalism. On the one hand, the national government, and particularly the federal judiciary, has taken important steps to protect individual rights against violation by state governments in such areas as freedom of speech, due process, and equal protection of the law. On the other hand, the national government frequently exercises its expanded powers in ways that are antithetical to individual liberty; and the courts, beginning with the *Darby* decision and continuing through more recent decisions such as *Garcia* (see chapter 1), have virtually eliminated the power of the states to protect against such abuses, as the Tenth Amendment intended them to do.

But federalism suffered an even greater casualty during this period: the disappearance of any principled defense of the doctrine. Whereas federalism had been intended as a mighty bulwark for individual liberty, it now was asserted as frequently against liberty as it was in favor of it. As a constitutional doctrine that had any meaning behind which Americans could proudly rally, federalism was dead.

The Emergence of the Local Leviathan

But if federalism was dead, local governments were not. To hear the cries of states' rights advocates, an observer would conclude that the enormous growth of the national government was accompanied by a serious atrophying among state and local governments. To the contrary, while the power of state and local governments has declined during the past 60 years relative to the power of the national government, in absolute terms the scope of state and local government power has expanded exponentially—as has the potential for that power to abuse individual rights.

In certain significant respects, the national government pales in comparison to the size and scope of local governments. Unlike the national government, local governments can multiply, and they do so in rabbit-like fashion. The number of local governments increased by as many as 4,000 during the 1970s alone[38]—a rate of more than one new local government created every single day— pushing the total number of local governments to more than 80,000.[39] Just like the federal government, local governments grew in size and influence, with each new bond issue, regulation, or ordinance accompanied by commensurate growth in local government budgets and employees. Indeed, with 500,000 elected and 13 million appointed officials, local government employees now outnumber civilian federal employees by nearly seven to one.[40] State budgets doubled from $258 billion in 1980 to $525 billion in 1989,[41] and the number of state employees grew more than twice as fast as the national population.[42]

Likewise, the explosive growth of the national regulatory apparatus from the New Deal onward has been paralleled at the state and local levels. Many federal regulatory agencies now are duplicated by agencies at the state and local levels. For instance, the counterparts of the federal Equal Employment Opportunity Commission include fair employment commissions at the state level and human rights commissions at the local level; other federal agencies regulating such concerns as commerce and the environment have similar counterparts. Often, these agencies replicate the efforts of others at different levels of government; sometimes they contradict one another, subjecting individuals and businesses to conflicting degrees of regulatory control.

In addition to the creation of regulatory agencies, new types of local governments have proliferated, subjecting individuals to government influence from new and different sources. These government units, known as "public authorities," are created by other government units, which delegate powers to the new entities. For instance, two or more local governments might form a "regional

[38]Thomas Anton places the number at 2,000; see Thomas J. Anton, *American Federalism and Public Policy* (New York: Random House, 1989), p. 6. Michael Libonati places the figure at 4,000; see Michael Libonati, "Home Rule: An Essay on Pluralism," *Washington Law Review* 64 (1989): 51, 52.

[39]Anton, p. 4; Libonati, p. 52.

[40]Anton, p. 4.

[41]Virginia I. Postrel, "The States Are Becoming the New 'Big Government,' " *Washington Post*, July 14, 1991, p. C3.

[42]Andrew Bates, "Blame Game," *New Republic*, November 4, 1991, p. 11.

authority" to operate regional transportation, or a city might form a "special district" to construct and maintain a sewer system. Often, these entities are operated as public corporations, with the idea that they will operate public services without the political influence and red tape of government. In fact, the opposite is often true: public authorities possess the inefficient attributes of government, but are not subject to democratic constraints. As Diana Henriques has observed in her study of public authorities entitled *The Machinery of Greed*,

> Whereas a corporate board of directors is chosen by and legally answerable to the stockholders, the public authority board of directors is generally appointed by some political official, perhaps with the consent of a legislative body. These public authority directors are only vaguely, if at all, accountable to the official who appointed them and are rarely required to answer to the public through an election or referendum.[43]

By 1985, more than one of every four local governments—26,000 in all—were of this variety, and they were growing in number far more rapidly than any other form of government.[44] Henriques observes that "the number of public authorities has been moving relentlessly upward every year," and may be "already the most numerous form of local government."[45]

Public authorities have dramatically expanded the role of government into day-to-day life, encompassing within their scope such matters as electricity, housing, water, airports, hospitals, roads, transportation, and sports. As a result, Henriques explains, public authorities "touch the lives of millions of Americans. . . . Only the rare American can make it through a day without encountering the work of some public authority."[46]

Most alarmingly, these new forms of local government possess sweeping powers such as eminent domain, taxation, and regulation.[47] But they are often obscured from public view and insulated

[43]Diana B. Henriques, *The Machinery of Greed* (Lexington, Mass.: Lexington Books, 1986), pp. 3–4.

[44]Anton, p. 4.

[45]Henriques, p. 5.

[46]Ibid., pp. 5–6.

[47]See, for example, Robert G. Smith, *Public Authorities in Urban Areas* (Washington: National Association of Counties, 1969).

78

from democratic processes. As Henriques observes, "Virtually all of [their] decisions are made in an atmosphere of unguided discretion."[48] The result of this dramatic expansion of the scope of government powers—in the hands of government bodies that are obscured from public scrutiny and insulated from democratic processes—is to render obsolete one of the basic tenets of the traditional concept of federalism: the belief that government is more controllable when it is closer to home.

In sum, the massive growth of local government during the past several decades is nothing less than phenomenal. Indeed, however awesome and lamentable the expansion of national government power in the past half-century, its impact on individual liberty is rivaled, if not surpassed, by the enormous expansion of government power at the local level.

Situational Federalism

As the nature and scope of local government has evolved, so the debate over federalism has changed over time. The battle lines are not as clear today as they were during the New Deal, or even in the early 1960s, when liberals controlled the national government and viewed states as impediments in the quest to establish a more ideal society. In those days, conservatives favored federalism, or at least the states' rights variety of federalism, while liberals did everything they could to consign federalism to the dustbin of history.

But two seminal events changed this previously reliable equation. First, the emergence of the local leviathan shifted allegiances somewhat. States and cities that were once guardians of the traditional society were evolving into social laboratories. That made liberals curious and conservatives nervous. Meanwhile, conservatives were gaining influence at the national level and were intent upon pursuing a deregulation agenda. That made liberals nervous and led conservatives to reconsider whether national power was altogether bad. This intra-ideological confusion has hastened the degeneration of federalism from a vital principle into an empty slogan invoked by whatever side happens to support states' rights in any given dispute.

[48]Henriques, p. 34.

The modern era of situational federalism (one's position on federalism depends upon whose policy agenda is advanced) traces its roots to the Nixon administration, which exhumed federalism while profoundly transforming it. President Richard Nixon was extremely distrustful of national government yet was an activist who often favored new government initiatives. He combined traditional federalism, in which local government is preferred because it is closer to the people, with modern liberal federalism, in which states act as social laboratories. As Timothy Conlan has recounted, "Nixon viewed his federalism strategy as a means of improving and strengthening government, especially at the state and local levels."[49] Nixon's federalism assigned the national government a coordinating role with respect to social and regulatory programs, but allowed state and local governments to implement them through the use of federal revenue sharing and block grants, with the net effect of decentralizing certain government programs while expanding their overall reach.

This model of federalism is the one that dominates among most social science academics today: the federal government furnishes funding and regulatory direction, while the more efficient state and local governments exercise considerable discretion in administering the programs. Theoretically, this contemporary model of federalism is more faithful to the original constitutional model of federalism, particularly in comparison to the New Deal and Great Society tendencies to centralize government authority, in that it removes some of that authority from the national government and places it in the hands of presumably more responsive local officials. But under this new distribution of government power, states act as agents of the national government, rather than as autonomous entities capable of acting on behalf of their citizens (as, for example, when western states attempted during the 1970s to resist federal efforts to impose a 55-mile-per-hour speed limit but learned that with federal money comes federal control). Hence the separation and balance of powers between the national and state governments, intended in the original design to check the power of both, is altogether missing from this new federalism.

[49]Timothy Conlan, *New Federalism* (Washington: Brookings Institution, 1988), p. 12.

Moreover, many of the local officials who administer "new federalism" programs are unaccountable bureaucrats rather than elected officials. As a result, whatever the distribution of power in this new system, the net result is vastly increased government, with slight (if any) reductions in the size of the national government, but enormous increases in the power of governments closer to home. If the purpose of decentralized government in a system of federalism is, as I have argued, to ensure that individuals have maximum control over their own affairs, the revival of federalism during the Nixon era had precisely the opposite effect.

After Nixon, few outside of social science circles gave much attention to federalism, until the election of Ronald Reagan in 1980. Brought to power by a profound popular reaction against big government, the Reagan administration was more genuinely interested in issues of federalism than any other in modern times. But the administration was also internally divided about the meaning of federalism and how to implement it. Virtually everyone in the administration wanted to reduce the size and power of the national government, but the administration was split over the use of national government power to reduce the size and scope of government at the local level. Stated differently, the two sides had different reasons for reducing national government power: for one side, the goal was to increase individual liberty, while the goal for the other side was to increase the autonomy of state and local governments. Those in the first camp tended to focus on economic issues, using deregulation and decentralization to promote a free-market economy, while the second group concentrated more on social issues and believed that local communities ought to possess the power to regulate community values. The free-market conservatives dominated such agencies as the Federal Trade Commission (FTC) and the Federal Communications Commission, while the states' rights conservatives were preeminent in the Department of Justice, particularly under Attorney General Edwin Meese. Both sides professed fidelity to the principles of federalism, and many in the administration straddled the divide between the two factions, coming down on one side or the other depending upon the desired policy outcome in any given instance. But the result was an administration that, although preoccupied with issues of federalism, failed to develop a unified theory of federalism and ultimately charted a tragically schizophrenic policy course on matters of federalism.

81

The way the Reagan administration implemented federalism often depended upon the outcome desired in a specific instance. Many of the administration's decisions were consistent with the protection of individual liberty, but rarely were they defended on the basis of any consistent view of federalism. For instance, Reagan's cuts in federal spending, Timothy Conlan has argued, were not designed primarily to enhance state and local governments, but instead "represent[ed] a reaction against fundamental elements of the welfare state." In Conlan's words:

> State and local government may have been preferred to federal involvement in many circumstances, but often only as a fallback to no governmental involvement whatsoever. In those cases where the federal policy appeared to give more free rein to private markets than state and local policies, the Reagan administration consistently endorsed preserving or enhancing the federal role—states' rights rhetoric notwithstanding.[50]

As additional examples of the Reagan administration's willingness to sometimes displace "states' rights," Conlan cites its use of the Fourteenth Amendment to challenge racial quotas and minority contract set-asides adopted by states and local governments, and its support for federal "preemption" of local economic regulations that were more restrictive than their federal counterparts.[51]

But these deregulatory actions by the national government are not, as Conlan has asserted, contrary to federalism. To the extent that the Reagan administration favored decentralization but used federal law to achieve such aims as free enterprise and racial neutrality, such efforts advanced traditional federalism principles because they applied federal law against the states only to promote individual liberty. The Fourteenth Amendment, for instance, forbids state governments from denying individuals equal protection of the laws, and gives power to the federal government to enforce that guarantee (see chapter 10). Conlan's second example, the federal preemption (that is, superseding) of state economic regulations, is

---

[50]Ibid., p. 99.
[51]Ibid., pp. 212–17.

an issue that divides many conservatives.[52] But the principal purpose of the national government's interstate commerce power is to prevent parochial state economic regulations that inhibit the free flow of interstate trade. Thus, it is fully consistent with federalism for the national government to preempt anticompetitive state regulations. Even Robert Bork defends the limited use of regulatory preemption against attacks by conservatives. "The fact that the pendulum has swung too far in the direction of centralization should not produce a knee-jerk hostility to federal power," argues Bork. "Much as some of us may deplore the misuse of that power, we must not fall into the opposite error of resisting its use on all occasions."[53]

Moreover, the use of federal tools to curb the power of state governments was not as common as Conlan asserts, in that such efforts were limited to a few specific policy areas. Indeed, many in the administration resisted actions, even in the area of economic regulation, that would restrict the power of state and local governments, and most of the administration's efforts were directed toward expanding, rather than restricting, the power of state and local governments.

The views of these states' rights conservatives were reflected in Executive Order 12612 in 1987. The executive order's stated objective was to

> restore the division of governmental responsibilities between the national government and the States that was intended by the Framers of the Constitution and to ensure that the principles of federalism established by the Framers guide the Executive departments and agencies in the formulation and implementation of policies.[54]

Section 2 of the executive order articulated "fundamental federalism principles":

> (a) Federalism is rooted in the knowledge that our political liberties are best assured by limiting the size and scope of the national government.

[52]See Paul Glastris, "All-American Brawl," *U.S.News & World Report*, June 10, 1991, p. 26; Charles Fried, *Order and Law* (New York: Simon & Schuster, 1991), pp. 186–88.

[53]Robert H. Bork, *Federalism and Federal Regulation: The Case of Product Labeling* (Washington: Washington Legal Foundation, 1991), p. 4.

[54]Preamble, Executive Order 12612 (October 26, 1987).

> (b) The people of the States created the national government when they delegated to it those enumerated governmental powers relating to matters beyond the competence of the individual States. All other sovereign powers, save those expressly prohibited the States by the Constitution, are reserved to the States or to the people. . . .
> (d) The people of the States are free, subject only to restrictions in the Constitution itself or in constitutionally authorized Acts of Congress, to define the moral, political, and legal character of their lives. . . .
> (e) In most areas of governmental concern, the States uniquely possess the constitutional authority, the resources, and the competence to discern the sentiments of the people and to govern accordingly.[55]

The executive order declared that the Tenth Amendment governs the relationship between the states and the national government, with the effect of limiting the powers of the national government to those explicitly enumerated, and of establishing a presumption of state sovereignty in the absence of clear constitutional or statutory authority.[56] To implement these principles, the executive order required federal agencies to closely examine the authority and need for any federal action "that would limit the policymaking discretion of the States," and to conduct a "federalism assessment" of the impact of all proposed regulations.[57] The order also established a presumption against findings of federal preemption of state regulatory actions (precisely opposite Conlan's thesis), and placed limits on any Reagan administration legislative proposals that would limit state powers.[58]

Executive Order 12612 is a classic statement of the states' rights view of federalism, in which the Tenth Amendment is exalted (correctly establishing a presumption in favor of state versus national power), but the Ninth Amendment (which establishes a presumption in favor of individual liberty against restrictions of liberty) is altogether ignored. The executive order was clearly

[55]Ibid., sec. 2.
[56]Ibid., sec. 2(c), (g), and (i).
[57]Ibid., sec. 3, 6.
[58]Ibid., sec. 4, 5.

intended by states' rights conservatives to restrain the efforts of free-market conservatives within the administration.

These two factions within the administration fought a spirited battle for the soul of federalism. Former solicitor general (now Harvard law professor) Charles Fried recounts that his efforts to counteract abuses by state and local governments were constantly scrutinized by the "federalism police" in the Reagan administration:

> The driving force behind their argument was the belief, widely held in the generation that had framed and ratified the Constitution, that strong local institutions were a bulwark of democracy and a protection against impositions by an arrogant, distant, and overreaching national government. I was not so sure. I feared the "village tyrant," an equally serious threat to individual liberty.[59]

The division within the administration between free-market and states' rights conservatives was perhaps best illustrated by the fight over enforcing federal antitrust laws against anticompetitive acts of municipalities. As the power of local governments has expanded, so has the tendency to use that power to restrict economic opportunities and bestow favoritism. In areas ranging from government-imposed taxicab monopolies to minimum milk price regulations to cable television franchising, local governments have imposed protectionist restrictions to benefit some (city agencies among them) to the detriment of others. Those anticompetitive acts are insulated from corrective market forces because they are enforced by government.

But until the late 1970s, the federal antitrust laws were completely unavailable to challenge such anticompetitive regulations, despite the devastating effect of those regulations upon the marketplace competition the antitrust laws were intended to enhance.[60] In a rare bow to states' rights federalism, the New Deal–era Supreme Court in *Parker* v. *Brown* ruled that states are immune from antitrust liability, upholding a state law designed to restrict competition in the raisin industry, which thereby artificially inflated prices—an

---

[59]Fried, pp. 186–87.

[60]I take no position on whether "enhancing" market competition, as the antitrust laws purportedly do, is an appropriate function of government at any level. At the least, however, restricting market efficiency, which is precisely what these regulations do, can hardly be an appropriate government function.

action that would violate antitrust laws if taken by a private business. Declaring that under our "dual system of government" the "states are sovereign," the Court declined to infer congressional intent to include states within the coverage of antitrust laws.[61] The ruling demonstrated that the liberal Court was willing to temporarily set aside its antipathy toward states' rights for the greater goal of stringent economic regulation.

But in 1978, the Court ruled in *City of Lafayette* v. *Louisiana Power & Light Co.* that state immunity under the antitrust laws did not automatically extend to cities. Dissenting from that holding, Justice Potter Stewart complained that the decision created an intolerable risk of liability for local governments, which "often take actions that might violate the antitrust laws if taken by private persons, such as granting exclusive franchises, enacting restrictive zoning ordinances, and providing public services on a monopoly basis."[62]

But for the Court's majority, that was exactly the point. As Justice William Brennan declared, local governments

> participate in and affect the economic life of this Nation in a great number and variety of ways. . . . [T]hey are fully capable of aggrandizing other economic units with which they interrelate, with the potential of serious distortion of the rational and efficient allocation of resources, and the efficiency of free markets which the regime of competition embodied in the antitrust laws is thought to engender. If municipalities were free to make economic choices counseled solely by their own parochial interests and without regard to their anticompetitive effects, a serious chink in the armor of antitrust protection would be introduced at odds with the comprehensive national policy Congress established.[63]

Four years later, in *Community Communications Co.* v. *City of Boulder*, the Court extended antitrust coverage to cities acting in their regulatory capacity, in the specific context of a challenge to an exclusive cable television franchise granted by the city. In dissent, Justice William Rehnquist warned that the decision would "impede,

[61]317 U.S. 341, 351 (1943).
[62]435 U.S. 389, 439 (1978) (Stewart, J., dissenting).
[63]Ibid., at 408 (majority).

if not paralyze, local governments' efforts to enact ordinances and regulations aimed at protecting public health, safety, and welfare."[64]

Free-market conservatives in the Reagan administration hailed the decisions, and the FTC filed lawsuits challenging city taxicab regulations in New Orleans and Minneapolis. But Congress, responding to intense pressure from the National League of Cities, cut off funds for the FTC prosecutions.[65] Meanwhile, states' rights conservatives positioned the Reagan administration behind legislation designed to curtail local government antitrust liability. The resulting law, signed by President Reagan in 1984, immunized local governments from monetary damages in antitrust cases, thus removing much of the potency of challenges to anticompetitive practices of local governments. Hence, the supposedly pro-free-market Reagan administration was responsible for all but eliminating one of the most effective weapons available to protect economic liberty against abuses inflicted by local governments.

Nor was this episode an aberration. In 1986, Attorney General Meese criticized a series of Supreme Court decisions that struck down state economic regulations that discriminated against out-of-state enterprises, contending that the decisions "curbed state power to regulate the economy"; while he applauded "the respect shown by the Court for state and local autonomy" in decisions limiting local government antitrust liability.[66] Meese went as far as to question the applicability of the Bill of Rights to the states.[67]

The internal debate over federalism within the Reagan administration—carried over, in perhaps less-pronounced form, into the Bush administration—will have long-lasting ramifications in that more than half the federal judiciary was appointed by those two presidents. In essence, the states' rights conservatives in the Reagan administration believed the national government to be virtually powerless to protect individuals against many of the most flagrant violations of liberty, as long as those violations were committed by

---

[64]455 U.S. 40, 60 (1982) (Rehnquist, J., dissenting).

[65]Nadine Cohodas, "Antitrust Relief for Cities Approved by House Judiciary," *Congressional Quarterly*, August 4, 1984, p. 1888.

[66]Edwin Meese III, speech before the American Bar Association, in *The Great Debate: Interpreting Our Written Constitution* (Washington: Federalist Society, 1986), p. 4.

[67]See Curtis, p. viii.

state or local governments. In particular, they believed the courts were guilty of judicial activism when they curbed excesses of state and local governments. This "idea that protection of human liberty under the Bill of Rights against state action is the result of judicial whim or judicial usurpation," Curtis has remarked, "eats like acid at the legitimacy of federal protection of civil liberty."[68] In sum, even as the rhetoric of the Reagan administration championed taking government off the backs of the people, many of its actions contradicted its rhetoric, thereby strengthening the ability of local governments to engage in grassroots tyranny.

States' Rights Liberalism

Meanwhile, as liberals watched their grip over the federal government—including the federal judiciary—slip away in the 1980s, they discovered the potential utility of state governments in advancing egalitarian objectives. As Conlan has noted, liberals "gained a new appreciation of federalism's segmented policymaking during the Reagan years."[69] What they could no longer accomplish at the national level, they could still achieve at the state and local level.

Social action federalism—deference to state and local governments when they are pursuing liberal objectives (see chapter 1)—is composed of two principal mechanisms. The first is deference by the federal judiciary, in the name of federalism, to experiments by state and local governments that otherwise might violate federal constitutional guarantees. A classic example is the liberals' remarkably contradictory Fourteenth Amendment jurisprudence, in which they consistently have stretched the scope of the amendment in areas such as desegregation, but have deferred to local autonomy on issues such as racial quotas and minority set-asides.[70]

[68]Ibid., pp. 2–3.

[69]Conlan, p. 236.

[70]Contrast, for example, Justice Brennan's Fourteenth Amendment jurisprudence in busing cases such as *Green* v. *County School Board of New Kent County*, 391 U.S. 430, 440 (1968), in which Brennan struck down a local school board's student assignment plan on the grounds that " 'freedom of choice' is not an end in itself," with racial preference cases, in which Brennan happily deferred to local autonomy even when exercised in a patently discriminatory fashion, holding quite remarkably that "no fundamental right is involved" in such cases. *Regents of the University of California* v. *Bakke*, 438 U.S. 265, 357 (Brennan, J., concurring in the judgment in part and dissenting in part). See also *Johnson* v. *Transportation Agency*, 480 U.S. 616 (1987), in which Brennan wrote the majority opinion.

The second mechanism is state court activism, in which state courts interpret selected provisions of the federal and state constitutions more broadly than do the federal courts. Analysts of social activism in the state courts observe that "for the past decade or so, partly in reaction to restrictive readings of constitutional rights by a more conservative federal judiciary, civil liberties lawyers have begun to look first" to state constitutions to achieve their goals.[71] State constitutions often provide fertile territory for the creation of new rights and responsibilities. The California state constitution, for instance, is more than twice as long as the U.S. Constitution, Magna Carta, Mayflower Compact, Declaration of Independence, and Articles of Confederation combined.[72]

Justice William Brennan, the principal architect of social action federalism, remarked that "rediscovery by state supreme courts of the broader protections afforded their own citizens by their state Constitutions . . . is probably the most important development in constitutional jurisprudence of our times."[73] Clothing the doctrine of state court activism in terms rarely invoked by liberals, Brennan insisted that "every believer in our concept of federalism, and I am a devout believer, must salute this development in our state courts."[74] But Brennan viewed state court activism as complementary to efforts in the past half-century to dramatically expand the role of the federal judiciary. "The legal revolution which has brought federal law to the fore," he declared, "must not be allowed to inhibit the independent protective force of state law."[75]

Sometimes such activism works in favor of individual liberty, but in many instances it undercuts liberty. Liberal state courts, for example, have transformed the constitutional guarantee of free speech from a restraint against government interference with speech into an affirmative entitlement. American Civil Liberties Union lawyer Margaret Crosby has argued, for instance, that "the free-speech issues of the 1990s" center on whether "less-affluent

[71]William Bennett Turner and Beth S. Brinkmann, "The Constitution of First Resort," *California Lawyer* (June 1989), p. 52.

[72]Ibid.

[73]Quoted in ibid., p. 54.

[74]William J. Brennan, Jr., "State Constitutions and the Protection of Individual Rights," *Harvard Law Review* 90 (1977): 489, 502.

[75]Ibid., p. 491.

speakers" will have a right to "subsidized speech" to get their messages across.[76]

This issue of "subsidized speech" provides a perfect illustration of social action federalism in practice. In a 1972 decision, the Supreme Court ruled that the First Amendment, which is a restraint solely upon government rather than private action, does not guarantee individuals the right to petition in a private shopping center.[77] As Justice Brennan later complained, "The Court has found the first amendment insufficiently flexible to guarantee access to essential public forums when in our evolving society those traditional forums are under private ownership in the form of suburban shopping centers."[78]

But all was not lost. In 1979, the California Supreme Court recognized precisely such a right of individuals to petition in private shopping centers.[79] When the shopping center's owners attempted to protect their own First Amendment and private-property rights in the U.S. Supreme Court, their pleas were rejected. In an opinion by Justice William Rehnquist, a states' rights conservative, the Court ruled that no free-speech violation occurred because the owners could disassociate themselves from the petitioners' message.[80] Furthermore, he wrote, even though "there literally has been a 'taking' " of the owners' "right to exclude others," it did not "unreasonably impair the value or use of their property as a shopping center."[81] Rehnquist fully embraced the doctrine of social action federalism, declaring that a state may "exercise its police power or its sovereign right to adopt in its own Constitution individual liberties more expansive than those conferred by the Federal Constitution."[82] An ebullient Justice Thurgood Marshall, concurring with Rehnquist, took the opportunity to "applaud the court's decision, which is a part of a very healthy trend of affording state

---

[76]Turner and Brinkmann, p. 52.

[77]*Lloyd Corp.* v. *Tanner*, 407 U.S. 551 (1972).

[78]Brennan, p. 496.

[79]*Robins* v. *PruneYard Shopping Center*, 23 C.3rd 899 (1979).

[80]*PruneYard Shopping Center* v. *Robins*, 447 U.S. 79, 87 (1980).

[81]Ibid., at 82–83.

[82]Ibid., at 81.

constitutional provisions a more expansive interpretation than this Court has given to the Federal Constitution."[83]

Social action federalism of this sort has enormous corrosive potential with respect to basic individual liberties such as freedom of speech, freedom of contract, private-property rights, and economic liberty—freedoms about which many liberals hold conflicting or contradictory positions, and freedoms that many conservatives are loath to protect if such protection conflicts with states' rights. Thus, the growing anomaly that a system intended to protect such freedoms is often manipulated to subvert those freedoms.

The Foundation for Grassroots Tyranny

The steady erosion of constitutional protections of individual liberty, combined with the absence of credible defenders of those liberties, has created ideal conditions in which grassroots tyranny can thrive. The growth in the number and power of local governments has produced myriad opportunities for abuses of power. The elimination of judicial restraints against such abuses, at the hands of conservatives and liberals alike, has greatly reduced the likelihood of effective deterrents against grassroots tyranny.

As Judge Alex Kozinski warned,

> Experience reinforces Madison's observation that at the lower levels of government it becomes much more likely "that measures [will be] too often decided, not according to the rules of justice and the rights of the minor party, but by the superior force of an interested and overbearing majority."[84]

The following chapters illustrate the prescience of Madison's warning.

The Framers of the Constitution—and the architects of the Fourteenth Amendment a century later—attempted to construct durable safeguards to protect our precious liberties against abuses by government. Those to whom the protection of these bulwarks of liberty was entrusted have too often abdicated their high responsibility, with the result that today our liberties are constantly in jeopardy.

[83]Ibid., at 91 (Marshall, J., concurring).

[84]*Associated General Contractors of California* v. *City & County of San Francisco*, 813 F.2d 922, 930 (9th Cir. 1987)(quoting *The Federalist* no.10 [Madison]).

Until we understand the true meaning of the constitutional principles that are our legacy as a nation—and the ramifications that
inevitably flow from departures from these principles—we cannot
fulfill their great promise, the promise of a nation of liberty.

PART II

GRASSROOTS TYRANNY

5. The Many Manifestations of Grassroots Tyranny

"You can't fight city hall."

One of the oldest expressions in American political life, yet also one of the most curious. The American sense of community is strong. Most typically, when a person thinks of his or her community, the image is of a town; or if a city, then of a particular neighborhood within the city. These small entities are the principal organic units in America, the places to which people feel the strongest attachment, the strongest sense of belonging and commitment.

But even in these small units, a chasm exists between the people and their governments. City halls, such as they are, seem distant, unresponsive, and even foreboding. Why is it that despite strong ties to their communities, people often feel alienated from their local governments?

The explanation lies in the distinction between "community" and "local government," which often are thought of as two sides of the same coin, but which are quite distinct. Communities are by their very nature formed around individuals who choose to create or join them. Local governments, conversely, are political entities whose jurisdictions are often arbitrary. The hallmark of community is voluntarism. In a true community, rules are set by mutual consent. As a result, individuals within communities may establish whatever rules they wish, because every member is free to choose whether or not to be a member of that community. On the other hand, government has coercive powers that do not rely on unanimous consent. To keep these powers in check, government in the American natural law tradition is supposed to respect certain fundamental individual rights. No matter how strong the consensus, there are certain limits of individual autonomy that government is bound to respect, at least theoretically.

In America's early years, local governments were often formed around true communities, in which all of the residents were united by religious values or common interests. Some of these governments were alter egos of the churches to which all residents belonged; others were town hall democracies, in which all citizens played a direct role in governance. By contrast, few local political units in America today are composed entirely of individuals who subscribe to common tenets. Hence, the true communities that exist today typically are not cities, towns, or counties, but more commonly are formed around religious institutions, neighborhood groups, social or ethnic clubs, and other entities consisting of individuals who voluntarily associate with one another for common purposes. The most important relationships that people form in their communities thus often have little to do with the geographical entity in which they live. As a result, the attachment people feel toward their communities, even when expressed in terms of a specific city or town, often does not manifest itself in any particular loyalty to the political entities that govern the communities.

If towns and cities consisted entirely of people who voluntarily joined together and universally subscribed to common tenets, city hall would not be an alien place, in that it would operate with the consent of everyone it governed. In reality, the rules that govern local communities are established not by the universal consent of the people who are governed, but at best by majoritarian political processes and at worst through narrow special-interest manipulation. In either case, there are winners and losers. If the winners stray beyond the boundaries appropriate to government—if they use the coercive power of government in ways that violate the rights of other people—government loses its legitimacy in the eyes of those whose rights are violated.

The unsavory reputation that "city hall" has earned over the years is precisely the consequence of what often happens when ordinary people obtain power over other people: that power is exercised not for the common good, but to benefit some at the expense of others. The abuse of power and the violation of individual rights by local governments is what constitutes grassroots tyranny.

Grassroots tyranny takes a wide variety of forms, many of which are well-known to most Americans. For example:

- Grassroots tyranny occurs when local government officials violate the public trust placed in them by using their positions for personal gain, wasting or misusing tax dollars, breaking promises, or otherwise placing their own interests above those of the people who elected them.

- Grassroots tyranny exists when the machinery of local government is used to impose a particular set of social values on people who do not subscribe to those values.
- Grassroots tyranny takes place when local government interferes with voluntary, nonharmful economic activities; when it violates private-property rights; and when it rearranges opportunities for the benefit of some and to the detriment of others.
- Grassroots tyranny occurs when local government impairs fundamental civil liberties such as freedom of speech, assembly, and religion, and the right to privacy.
- Grassroots tyranny exists when local government goes beyond vigorous law enforcement and heavy-handedly violates the precious personal liberties guaranteed by the Bill of Rights.

The list could go on and on.

The enormous power of local government is a force most people do not comprehend until it impacts them personally. Despite its vast scope and oppressive potential, local authority often escapes critical attention from the individuals it was created to serve, as well as from those branches of government entrusted with checking abuses of government power, principally the judiciary (a phenomenon whose origins are explored in the preceding chapters).

But although they often escape scrutiny, instances of grassroots tyranny are plentiful, and have multiplied as the power and scope of local government have expanded. Where local governments at one time performed only the most basic public services, today they do everything from operating cable television stations and sewage treatment facilities to imposing rent control and taking positions on foreign policy issues. Virtually no aspect of moral, social, economic, or political life in America today is beyond the scope of local government.

Although many Americans feel an almost nostalgic attachment to the towns and cities in which they live, the specter of grassroots tyranny is omnipresent, and where it strikes it can destroy the sense of security and belonging that is essential to the concept of community. The clout of local government is enormous, and when abused, it can have a devastating impact on individuals—sometimes more so, in fact, than abuses of power at higher levels of government. Local governments tend to affect the lives of individuals much more directly, through taxation, control of public schools, regulation of property and businesses, and law enforcement. Yet, the officials who wield local government powers are typically far less visible than national officials. The local zoning or planning board commissioner, the school board member, the police commissioner—each possesses tremendous power over individuals in the community. Often, however, these government officials are unelected, largely unaccountable, and nearly invisible to the people over whom they exercise authority.

These factors are buttressed by the wide dispersion of local government powers among a wide variety of entities and officials. As a result, individuals are subject to a multiplicity of authorities regulating their lives and day-to-day affairs. In addition to state, county, and city governments, most citizens are taxed and regulated by one or more boards of education, special districts, and regional authorities. The sheer volume of local governments is remarkable. As of 1985, more than 82,000 separate units of local government were in existence. Included among this number were 40,000 municipal governments (cities, counties, etc.), 15,000 school districts, and 26,000 special districts. These entities encompassed 500,000 elected officials and 13 million employees—more than six times the number of federal civilian employees.[1]

There exists a broad array of government agencies and quasi-government entities that possess the powers but rarely the limits of elected government entities. They are the places where the fabled "nameless, faceless bureaucrats" reign, exercising enormous control over individual citizens while largely hidden from view and only indirectly accountable to the public. These agencies and boards regulate virtually every area of economic life and many areas of social life as well, from property development to entry into trades and professions to advertising—and even to what we watch on cable television. Although the size of constitutionally established governments (such as legislatures and city councils) is generally

---

[1] Thomas J. Anton, *American Federalism and Public Policy* (New York: Random House, 1989), p. 4.

finite, the size of the unelected bureaucracy is not, which means that most of the growth of local government is occurring in these nondemocratic entities. The result is a constant expansion in the amount of government power that is beyond the direct control of the citizenry, rendering local democratic processes largely impotent in curbing abuses of power.

Demonstrating the axiom that there is strength in numbers, local governments have combined with one another (and with allies such as public employee unions) to develop a potent special-interest lobby, which exercises enormous clout at the national level through lobbying organizations such as the National League of Cities. As urban studies scholar Thomas J. Anton has observed, "Local governments and their associated interests are powerful forces," constantly "on guard against efforts to weaken their authority."[2] The whole of the local government lobby is thus definitely greater, and far more powerful, than the sum of its parts.

Indeed, beyond championing the parochial interests of its members on specific issues, the local government lobby is also the leading proponent of an evolving concept of federalism that glorifies states and cities as social laboratories. This concept, of course, promotes greater local government autonomy and increased federal funding—the two prizes most valued by the local government lobby.

In sum, local government in its various permutations and combinations is all too often cumbersome, expensive, inefficient, uncontrollable, and oppressive. Its scope and its impact are awesome. When even the tiniest school districts have budgets totaling in the tens of millions of dollars, when a homeowner who wants to add a room to her house has to spend years of her life and penetrate multiple layers of bureaucracy to obtain approval, when unelected officials can obligate taxpayers to huge public bonds to finance sports arenas—it all demonstrates just how completely we have abandoned the model of town hall democracy. As Diana Henriques, a chronicler of grassroots tyranny, has put it, "How is an ordinary citizen to make sense of it all?"[3]

---

[2]Ibid., p. 6.

[3]Diana B. Henriques, *The Machinery of Greed* (Lexington, Mass.: Lexington Books, 1986), p. 35.

This is the soil in which grassroots tyranny thrives.

The next several chapters describe specific instances of grassroots tyranny in a variety of contexts. They illustrate some of the many ways in which local governments violate individual rights, sometimes acting at the behest of the people themselves or through those who are elected or appointed to carry out the powers of government. The overall picture that emerges is alarming and often heart-wrenching.

Grassroots tyranny takes a wide variety of forms. Sometimes it does not pit the government against specific individuals, but takes a more generalized form in which local government violates the rights of the members of the community as a whole. Perhaps the most common example of generalized grassroots tyranny is the abuse of tax dollars. Government officials operate, in a sense, as trustees for the public of funds raised by taxation. But few could survive the scrutiny to which ordinary trustees are subjected. Instances of misuse of public funds are common; indeed, probably only a small fraction are ever discovered.

To cite just one among myriad examples, in 1980, University of California president David Saxon spent $40,000 in public funds to campaign against a voter initiative designed to cut state income taxes. At taxpayer expense, Saxon sent a letter to the parents of every college student in the state's university system, warning (incorrectly) that the initiative would compel massive tuition increases, and stating that he was doing everything in his power to defeat the initiative. Saxon's scare tactics contributed significantly to the initiative's defeat at the polls. The use of taxpayer funds to defeat a taxpayer initiative illustrates the sheer arrogance of many unelected officials that fuels the abuse of public funds.

A related abuse is corruption, to which local government seems especially susceptible. In 1989, 71 officials at the state level were indicted in federal corruption investigations.[4] In South Carolina alone, 14 lawmakers were indicted on drug and bribery charges resulting from a Federal Bureau of Investigation (FBI) sting operation relating to a racetrack bill; by early 1991, half of the 14 had

---

[4]Gwen Ifill, "Scandals Cast New Light on Statehouse Ethics," *Washington Post*, February 24, 1991, p. A3.

pleaded guilty.[5] In Tennessee, an FBI investigation of the state's bingo industry led to corruption convictions of two state officials and the suicides of two others.[6] These reported incidents barely begin to tell the full story about the many state and local public officials—from building inspectors to police officers to governors— who abuse positions of public trust for personal gain.

The problems of local tax abuses and corruption are exacerbated by the proliferation of government entities that are shielded from public view, such as special districts and regional authorities, which often take in massive amounts of money and exercise sweeping powers even though they are insulated from democratic processes. As Diana Henriques observes in *The Machinery of Greed*, "Public authorities are not very visible agencies of government. . . . Many do not conduct public meetings or open their records to the press or the public. . . . There is not even any reliable way of identifying all the thousands of public authorities that exist in the country."[7] Yet, most "are subject to very little control or attention from the government units that created them."[8] For these reasons, Henriques concludes, public authorities "possess a structure, an environment, and a seclusion that makes them particularly prone to corruption."[9]

Henriques documents scandals involving three dozen public authorities. Such scandals are not surprising given that public authorities, as Henriques describes them, are "the most invisible critters in the political landscape."[10] In 1980, for instance, the *Baltimore Sun* reported the startling revelation that "the traditional city government had been nearly supplanted by a network of mayoral corporations" (that is, public corporations established by the mayor).[11] These public authorities

> were doing the public business with mostly public funds but were doing it in secret. Mayoral corporations were

[5]Ibid.
[6]Ibid.
[7]Henriques, p. 34.
[8]Ibid., p. 32.
[9]Ibid., p. 132.
[10]Ibid.
[11]Ibid.

> running city facilities, lending money to private builders, buying and reselling land, bailing out shaky private projects—all with few accurate records, few public hearings, little competitive bidding, primitive fiscal controls, and scant attention to federal, state, or city regulations.[12]

Yet, few Baltimore residents, including some members of the city council, "even knew that the corporations existed."[13] The people had lost control of their government; indeed, they had lost sight of it altogether.

Typical of oppressive regional authorities are the California air pollution control districts, which are unelected regional bodies that make and enforce air quality regulations. As attorney Robert J. Ernst reports, "Few Californians realize that their two-tiered system of state and local government no longer really exists. The air district and other super-regional agencies . . . have quietly supplanted Sacramento and local government, deciding the important issues without accountability."[14] The air districts create air standards, levy fines, and charge fees with little public input or due process. The Monterey Bay Unified Air Pollution Control District, policing an area that never has had any air pollution problems, has imposed regulations even more stringent than Los Angeles.[15] Its $5.7 million annual budget—collected from fines, business permit fees, sewer district and city assessments, and motor vehicle license fees—includes more than a quarter million dollars for lobbying and public relations.[16] With few limits on the size, scope, and powers of these new forms of government, there is little wonder that corruption thrives and is increasingly immune from the corrective influence of the ballot box.

Grassroots tyranny often takes much more direct forms, involving outright violations of individual rights. The next several chapters present a variety of direct forms of grassroots tyranny, but several others deserve brief discussion here.

[12]Ibid.

[13]Ibid.

[14]Robert J. Ernst III, "Clean Air's Dirty Politics," *American Spectator* (October 1992), p. 46.

[15]Ibid.

[16]Ibid.

Perhaps the most notorious type of abuse visited upon individuals by local government officials is police misconduct. Several of the rights explicitly guaranteed by the Bill of Rights were designed to protect individuals against police abuses,[17] but these protections are increasingly being eroded by a hostile Supreme Court.

Few people would question the difficulty of law enforcement, and most Americans are properly outraged over the procedural technicalities that often let criminals go free and victims uncompensated.[18] But in the process of enforcing the law, the police are not free to run roughshod over the very rights they are charged with protecting. The balance is a delicate but vitally important one, for with the badge of authority comes the power, if abused, to terrorize, oppress, and inflict grave harm.

In our modern society, instances of outright police brutality should be waning, but evidence exists that egregious police misconduct continues. The 1992 Los Angeles riots were sparked at least in part by the pent-up outrage that exists over police brutality in the inner city, as well as over the justice system's failure to effectively deter or punish brutality. The incident that triggered the riots occurred in March 1991, when a group of Los Angeles police officers brutally beat 25-year-old Rodney King, who was apprehended after a high-speed car chase. King was menacing but unarmed. As he lay prone and helpless, three of the officers kicked him and struck him with nightsticks at least 56 times as their sergeant and other officers looked on. King's leg was broken and his face was disfigured.

King's experience attracted national attention only because the beating was videotaped by a bystander. Apparently the incident was not an aberration; an independent commission that investigated the King incident found that a "significant number of LAPD officers . . . repeatedly misuse force" without receiving proper

[17]For example, the Third Amendment (prohibition against quartering of soldiers in homes), the Fourth Amendment (prohibition against unreasonable searches and seizures and requirement of warrants), and the Fifth Amendment (prohibition against deprivations of life, liberty, or property without due process of law).

[18]Indeed, personal security is the most fundamental civil right, and its protection is the most important role of government. See Clint Bolick, *Changing Course: Civil Rights at the Crossroads* (New Brunswick, N.J.: Transaction Books, 1988), pp. 116–18.

103

discipline.[19] The local chapter of the American Civil Liberties Union reports 50 calls a week complaining of police abuse.[20] Between 1978 and 1991, 27 people died from chokeholds applied by Los Angeles police.[21]

Other police methods used around the country are also often excessive. For instance, the frequent use by police of nunchuks (a martial arts weapon originally used by Asian farmers to control livestock) and other "pain compliance" methods in the arrests of nonviolent antiabortion protesters has led to serious injuries.[22]

Other forms of police misconduct are more subtle yet equally destructive of individual liberty, and such incidents increase as the scope of police power expands deeper into the private realm. In 1991, the U.S. Supreme Court upheld the power of police officers to board public buses, without probable cause to believe any crime was committed, to question passengers and search their luggage for illegal drugs. In August 1985, two Broward County, Florida, sheriff's deputies boarded a bus en route from Miami to Atlanta. Finding passenger Terrance Bostick asleep, one of the officers tapped Bostick on the foot to awaken him and asked if they could search his luggage. Bostick acquiesced. The officers found cocaine, and Bostick was sentenced to five years in prison for drug trafficking.[23]

Although the search ostensibly was voluntary, the specter of police intimidation was ominously present. The Florida Supreme Court overturned the conviction and struck down the practice of random searches on public buses, reasoning that

> roving patrols, random sweeps, and arbitrary searches or seizures would go far to eliminate . . . crime in this state.

[19]See, for example, Sonia L. Nozario and David J. Jefferson, "LA Law: A Videotaped Beating Highlights Problems of Los Angeles Police," *Wall Street Journal*, March 12, 1991, pp. A1 and A6; and Jay Mathews, "L.A. Police Probe Cites Bias, Misuse of Force," *Washington Post*, July 10, 1991, p. A1.

[20]Ibid.

[21]Ibid.

[22]See, for example, William B. Allen, "Police Brutality—but No Outrage," *Wall Street Journal*, August 18, 1989; Nat Hentoff, "The Painful Education of a Schoolteacher," *Washington Post*, September 2, 1989, p. A25; and Nat Hentoff, "Controlling the 'Pain Police,' " *Washington Post*, September 30, 1989, p. A21.

[23]Ruth Marcus, "Court to Scrutinize Random Questioning of Bus, Train Passengers," *Washington Post*, February 26, 1991, p. A5.

Nazi Germany, Soviet Russia, and Communist Cuba have demonstrated all too tellingly the effectiveness of such methods. Yet we are not a state that subscribes to the notion that ends justify means.[24]

But the U.S. Supreme Court disagreed and by a 6-3 vote overturned the Florida decision. Writing for the majority, Justice Sandra Day O'Connor declared that "this court is not empowered to forbid law enforcement practices simply because it considers them distasteful."[25] Unfortunately, by finding such random searches merely "distasteful" and not unconstitutional, the Court diminished the value of constitutional guarantees that protect the privacy of all Americans.

Another fundamental right that is in serious peril is the right to free exercise of religion, one of the foremost liberties protected by the Bill of Rights. The Supreme Court recently struck a tremendous blow against religious liberty in *Employment Division* v. *Smith*, ruling that the State of Oregon could prohibit the use of the drug peyote by Native Americans in religious rituals.[26] The use of the drug was voluntary, limited, and harmless both to the users and to others in the community. But the Court went beyond allowing the state to forbid this sacred religious practice. It silently overturned decades of case precedents and announced a new rule that could severely limit religious liberty in many other contexts. Henceforth, as long as the challenged government regulation is not aimed at religion and affects only religious practices, not beliefs, a law of general applicability is valid regardless of its impact on religious liberty. Because an essential purpose of protecting freedom of religion is to allow religious minorities to dissent from majoritarian orthodoxy, the *Smith* decision could have an enormously harmful impact on the practices of religious minorities.[27]

For instance, if construed broadly, the *Smith* decision might overturn the Supreme Court's landmark 1972 ruling in *Wisconsin* v.

---

[24]Quoted in ibid.

[25]Quoted in Michael Isikoff, "Court Allows Bus Search By Police Seeking Drugs," *Washington Post*, June 21, 1991, p. A10.

[26]110 S.Ct. 1595 (1990).

[27]See generally Ruth Marcus, "Reins on Religious Freedom?" *Washington Post*, March 9, 1991, p. A1.

Yoder, which held that the Amish had the right to refuse to send their children to high school in violation of the state's compulsory school attendance law.[28] The Court found that the state's interest in compulsory formal education of youngsters beyond a certain age was not sufficient to overcome the religious beliefs of the Amish that impelled them to dissent from that rule.[29] If this careful balancing of the state's interests and the individual's religious liberty is abandoned in favor of the *Smith* rule that allows enforcement of any generally applicable law—regardless of the need for the law or its impact on religious liberty—it could destroy a vital aspect of the religious liberty that the First Amendment is designed to protect.

Local governments have a negative impact on individual autonomy not only in their violation of fundamental rights but in the way they exercise control over public services. Nowhere are the consequences of misguided local public policy more pervasive and debilitating than in the area of education. The public school monopoly accounts for the greatest share by far of local public spending, but taxpayers and parents are often powerless to influence the quality or direction of the schools. Public schools frequently are expensive, ineffective, inefficient, and unresponsive; they inculcate values that many people find abhorrent.[30] And they are manipulated by what is perhaps the most potent and reactionary special-interest lobby in America, the National Education Association and its education establishment allies. The current system is particularly devastating for low-income youngsters, who lack the means to opt out of defective and dangerous public schools—schools that reinforce the cycle of poverty and despair rather than providing the tools for escaping it.[31] As long as public education remains an entrenched monopoly dominated by special interests, it will limit meaningful choice and competition, particularly for those youngsters who most need high-quality education. As a result, the grassroots tyranny visited by the public school monopoly is especially debilitating.

[28]*Wisconsin* v. *Yoder*, 406 U.S. 205 (1972).

[29]Ibid.

[30]See, for example, Stephen Arons, *Compelling Belief: The Culture of American Schooling* (New York: New Press, 1983).

[31]See, for example, David Boaz, ed., *Liberating Schools: Education in the Inner City* (Washington: Cato Institute, 1991).

Given the abundant examples of grassroots tyranny from which to choose, the subject matter of the following chapters is necessarily highly selective. However, each category profiled therein shares common characteristics. Each category—private property, freedom of speech, economic liberty, privacy, and equality under law—involves rights that are generally considered fundamental to American citizenship. Yet, in each of these areas, state and local governments persistently intrude upon those rights. And the consequences of such government intrusions are often extremely destructive to individual liberty.

The relative offensiveness of the particular intrusions is also a subjective matter; individuals certainly will disagree over whether the government has truly overstepped its proper bounds in specific instances. Moreover, many of these abuses of government power, though offensive, are probably legal. Indeed, some of the most egregious examples of grassroots tyranny are sanctioned not only by a majority acting through democratic processes, but by the judiciary as well. In a free society, however, such sanctions do not necessarily render abuses of government power any less abhorrent.

The purpose in presenting specific examples of grassroots tyranny is not to seek agreement about whether all, some, or merely a few of these examples represent abuses of government power. Rather, the purpose is to illustrate how far the pendulum has swung from the days when local governments were guardians of individual rights to today, when they far more commonly violate individual rights. I do not mean to disparage local government as such, but to sound an alarm over the danger to individual liberty that arises when the powers of local government are wielded in an arbitrary or oppressive manner. In sum, these abuses demonstrate the need to rethink a philosophy of federalism that today serves as a justification, if not as an outright shield, for such abuses to occur.

Fortunately, individuals are not defenseless against grassroots tyranny. The ballot box remains the most potent deterrent against abuses of government power, regardless of the level of government at which such abuses occur. But democratic processes are not always effective against tyranny visited by the majority upon the minority, or against tyranny that is shielded from public scrutiny or inflicted by government entities that are not directly accountable to the electorate (and the vast majority are not).

Where democratic processes fail to constrain grassroots tyranny, the courts are entrusted with the role of protecting individual rights. Indeed, they were designed to act as the ultimate safeguard of liberty, invested with the power to strike down unconstitutional laws, and with life tenure ensuring the independence of judges.[32] Additional safeguards were added in civil rights laws enacted after the Civil War, which gave individuals the right to challenge deprivations of federally protected rights "under color of state law" (42 U.S.C. § 1983). These laws also provide criminal penalties for willful violations of rights by state government officials (18 U.S.C. § 242). Since 1978, the courts have applied section 1983 to restrain violations of individual rights by local government officials.[33] But the courts do not always reliably serve their intended function as guardians of individual rights; indeed, the outcome in a particular case often depends on the value that the particular court places on the rights involved.

Certainly no presumption exists in contemporary American jurisprudence favoring individual autonomy over government power. To the contrary, the courts often serve not as a counterweight against majoritarian excesses but as a catalyst for such excesses. In such instances, alternative deterrents to grassroots tyranny include the media; local watchdog organizations, including taxpayer and civil liberties groups; and individuals willing to stand up for their rights. One need only recall the 1950s and 1960s—the boycott of public transit in Montgomery, Alabama, and the sit-ins and protests against segregated universities—to appreciate the efficacy and moral potency of civil disobedience in challenging abuses of individual rights by state and local governments. When democratic processes failed to vindicate the right of people to be free from government-enforced segregation, individuals stood together in common cause. Through persistent and principled struggle, they toppled a system of oppression perpetuated for a century by southern legislatures and city halls.

These experiences demonstrate that, in the final analysis, sunshine is the only antidote to grassroots tyranny. Whether outrage

---

[32]See Bolick, pp. 122–41. The view of the constitutional Framers of the courts being the ultimate protectors of individual rights is set forth in *The Federalist* no. 78 (Hamilton), in *The Federalist Papers* (New York: Modern Library, 1937).

[33]*Monnell* v. *Department of Social Services*, 436 U.S. 658 (1978).

over specific instances of grassroots tyranny incites a particular community to topple a corrupt or oppressive local government, inspires a popular movement to reclaim government from unelected bureaucrats, encourages a public-spirited lawyer to challenge the unchallengeable, or emboldens a single individual to stand up for his or her rights—that is the purpose of shedding light on these abuses.

Fighting city hall is a daunting enough task. Taming the local leviathan in its entirety and returning to individuals a greater measure of personal autonomy is a mammoth task—one that starts with understanding the nature of the beast. But in taking on such a challenge, we can draw inspiration from Thomas Paine, who observed in the context of an earlier struggle against oppressive government: "Tyranny, like hell, is not easily conquered; yet we have this consolation with us, the harder the conflict, the more glorious the triumph.[34]

---

[34]Thomas Paine, *The American Crisis*, no. 1 (1776).

6. Private Property

The beginning of the end of Nick and Helen Tokarczyk's happy life came in March 1981, when they received a letter telling them that the city of Detroit was buying their house.[1] That surprised them, since the house wasn't on the market and they wanted to continue living there. But the city had other ideas: the Tokarczyks were ordered to turn over their property to the city within 90 days.

The Tokarczyks were incredulous. At age 66, Nick Tokarczyk had no desire to leave the old ethnic Detroit neighborhood of Poletown, or the building that housed the Tokarczyks' residence along with a second apartment, two stores, a garage, and their livelihood, the Chene-Adele Bar. The couple had started renting the building 19 years before, and after 13 years had finally saved enough cash to make a down payment to buy it. Now the mortgage was paid off and the Tokarczyks wanted to live out their lives there. "We built this up for our old age," said Mr. Tokarczyk. "I never dreamed they would throw me out."

The city was forcing the Tokarczyks out to make way for a new General Motors (GM) Cadillac plant. GM had announced it was closing two outmoded factories but would build a new facility in Detroit if a suitable 500-acre site was made available. With unemployment at 18 percent, the city eagerly obliged, offering to buy and improve a tract in and around the Poletown neighborhood for $200 million, which in turn it would sell to GM for $8 million.

It was a great deal for GM, but not so good for the Tokarczyks or their neighbors in soon-to-be-obliterated Poletown, which was home to 3,500 residents, 150 businesses, 16 churches, and a hospital. To make matters worse, the city told the Tokarczyks it would pay them only $48,000 for their property —about half its appraised value.

---

[1] The following account is based primarily on Sheldon Richman, "The Rape of Poletown," *Inquiry*, August 3 & 24, 1981, pp. 11–12.

The city was exercising its power of eminent domain: the power to take private property for public use with "just compensation." Eminent domain is one of the most awesome powers of government, yet also one of the most frequently exercised. Regardless of the arbitrariness or unfairness of the decision, ordinary citizens usually possess neither the resources nor the time to do much more than quibble over the amount of "reasonable" compensation the government must pay.

Efforts to save Poletown, as writer Sheldon Richman has described them, were "doomed from the start."[2] Induced by declining police, fire, and garbage services, 90 percent of the neighborhood's residents agreed right away to sell their homes to the city. But the Tokarczyks and several of their neighbors refused to do so and waged a valiant counteroffensive. Forming the Poletown Neighborhood Council, they teamed up with Ralph Nader—not ordinarily an advocate of private-property rights but a bitter adversary of GM—and challenged the seizure of their property in court.

The principal constitutional restraints on government's power to interfere with private-property rights are found in the Fifth Amendment, which provides that ". . . nor shall private property be taken for public use, without just compensation" (the takings clause), and in the Fourteenth Amendment, which prohibits states from depriving people of property without due process of law.

The residents reasoned that because the beneficiary of the city's plans was GM, the seizure of the property was invalid in that it was for private rather than public use. But the Michigan Supreme Court disagreed. "The power of eminent domain is to be used in this instance to accomplish the essential public purposes of alleviating unemployment and revitalizing the economic base of the community," wrote Chief Justice Mary Coleman for the 5-2 majority. "Where there is such a public need, 'the abstract right [of an individual] to make use of his own property in his own way is compelled to yield to the general comfort and protection of the community.' "[3]

For the Tokarczyks and their neighbors, the impact of the city's actions was anything but "abstract." They lost their homes, their

[2]Ibid.
[3]Quoted in ibid., p. 12.

livelihoods—everything they had worked and saved for. Few people probably comprehend the power of eminent domain unless they personally are affected by it. Yet, apart from the requirement of compensation, it is virtually without limit, and is often exercised with little heed for the lives that are destroyed along with the property rights. As Sheldon Richman argues,

> The sacrifice of some people to "public need" is a shameful euphemism for the subordination of the rights of these people to the power of others. The travesty here is not that GM is the beneficiary, but that land is being stolen. Eminent domain, for *any* purpose, is contrary to the principles of a free society.[4]

The sacrifice of Poletown to "save" Detroit had unhappy endings all around: GM decided not to build the factory after all.

In a sense, the Tokarczyks and their neighbors were lucky, since they at least received some compensation for their loss, even though they would rather not have given up their property at any price. Many other property owners, by contrast, lose their property rights not through outright seizure by the government but through regulation that severely restricts the use or enjoyment of their property. In such situations, courts typically do not require any compensation at all.

Only recently has the U.S. Supreme Court begun to rein in over-zealous local governments, in a series of decisions culminating in its 1992 decision in *Lucas* v. *South Carolina Coastal Council*.[5] In 1986, David Lucas bought two beachfront lots on the Isle of Palms in South Carolina for $975,000. The lots were in a residential area, and Lucas intended to build a house for himself on one and another house to sell on the other. Two years later, the state enacted the Beachfront Management Act, limiting construction in certain beach areas ostensibly for environmental reasons. Under the new law, Lucas would be able to build nothing on his land. The value of his

---

[4]Ibid. (emphasis in original). Adding further irony, a few years later, Sheldon Richman, the writer who chronicled the Poletown tragedy, lost his own Fairfax County, Virginia, home to the power of eminent domain when county officials decided it was in the way of a highway they wanted to build.

[5]*Lucas* v. *South Carolina Coastal Council*, 112 S.Ct. 2886 (1992).

property—on which he still had to pay taxes and carry insurance—was reduced overnight from $1.2 million to virtually nothing.[6]

Lucas filed a lawsuit arguing that the state had taken his land and owed him compensation. The state contended that Lucas should bear the financial burden because the regulations did not amount to a taking of his property, and the regulations legitimately served the public interest. The South Carolina Supreme Court agreed with the state.

Fortunately for Lucas, the U.S. Supreme Court overturned the South Carolina court's ruling. Any time the government deprives landowners of the full value of their property, the Court declared, it must pay compensation unless the use of the property would amount to a nuisance.

Although the decision was a triumph for private-property rights, it may not prove far-reaching. What about regulations that deprive the owner of most of the property value, but not all? Will clever local governments leave property owners a small portion of the value of their property so as to thwart the obligation to pay "just compensation"?

The *Lucas* case shows how onerous regulations, as well as outright seizures of property by government, can severely diminish property rights. People's lives can be turned upside down by remarkably extreme local government regulations, as happened in the case of Ellen and Jerrold Ziman.

An observer looking at the behavior of the Zimans over a period of several years would find it bizarre. Why would a couple who had exhausted their life savings to purchase a $280,000 four-story home cram themselves and their two children into just two rooms of it? Why would they allow strangers whose lifestyles threatened the safety and well-being of the Ziman children to live in their home? Finally, why would the couple take on the obligations of landlords, which neither of them wanted?

The explanation for this strange behavior? Like thousands of other property owners, Ellen and Jerrold Ziman were caught in New York City's rent-control trap. Despite having consulted lawyers to make sure their seemingly simple plan to buy and live in their home was permissible under the law, the Zimans wound up

---

[6]Marcia Coyle, "Property Revival," *National Law Journal*, January 27, 1992.

spending $100,000 in legal fees and six years of their lives to extricate themselves from the regulatory miasma. Yet, comparatively speaking, they were fortunate. Untold others have been forced to sell their property at a loss or even abandon it owing to the perverse effects of rent-control laws. At least the Zimans ultimately got to keep their property and actually derive some benefit from it.

The Zimans' story started in 1984 when they purchased a 200-year-old Federal townhouse on a quiet Greenwich Village street for their family home.[7] Although the building was then divided into seven small apartments, lawyers assured the Zimans that local law permitted the eviction of the remaining three tenants, since the Zimans wished to occupy the building as their primary residence.

But in New York City, where the concept of property rights was long ago eclipsed by that of tenants' rights, nothing is a sure bet for property owners. Officials of the Department of Housing Conservation and Renewal (DHCR), the agency that administers the city's rent regulations, contended that the Zimans "should have known the legislature might change the law." And change it the legislators did. A mere four months after the Zimans purchased the property, and while eviction proceedings against the tenants were still pending, the legislature passed a law banning the eviction by owner-occupants of tenants who had lived in their apartments for 20 or more years. The law, which in effect granted such tenants the right to occupy their apartments for life, was effective immediately and applied to all pending eviction applications.

The Zimans' recalcitrant tenants were no doubt gleeful. Two immediately qualified for protection and the third had only a short time to go. Among the three of them, they were paying, under the provisions of New York City's rent-control law, a whopping $440 per month in rent.

Meanwhile, the Zimans were shelling out $450 per month just in property taxes, not to mention having to make their mortgage payment. In addition, they were forced to perform the services and

---

[7]The following account is based primarily on Carolyn Lochhead, "Live-in Nightmare on Dream Street," *Insight*, February 26, 1990, pp. 22–24; and Gordon Crovitz, "What's New in Greenwich Village? Property Rights," *Wall Street Journal*, June 13, 1990, p. A15. See also William Tucker, *Zoning, Rent Control, and Affordable Housing* (Washington: Cato Institute, 1991); and idem, *The Excluded Americans: Homelessness and Housing Policies* (Washington: Regnery Gateway, 1990).

take on the responsibilities of landlords, despite having no desire to do so. Worst of all, their inability to evict their holdout tenants prevented them from using the property as they had planned.

The Zimans had intended to restore the modest 1,590-square-foot building as a single-family home, with separate bedrooms for their two children and a master bedroom for themselves. Instead, they were forced to live entirely in just two rooms. One room served as a combined kitchen, dining room, living room, and bedroom for Mr. and Mrs. Ziman, while the other served as a bedroom for the children. Under these conditions, Mr. and Mrs. Ziman had no privacy and had to give up cooking and entertaining in their home. If one of their children had a playmate over, they would have to take their other child out for the day just to make room.

Concern for safety added to the problem. The Zimans' tenants apparently had distributed building keys to their friends. The tenants' guests freely entered the building and occasionally left the gate or door open behind them. The building was twice broken into while the Zimans lived there. Mr. Ziman also smelled marijuana in the hall and found a cocaine spoon on the second floor.

Eventually one of their tenants died, enabling the Zimans to transform his apartment into a bedroom for their son. But that proved a mixed blessing. To enter his bedroom, the nine-year-old boy had to climb the building's public stairs, unlock his bedroom door, and then lock it behind him.

This situation persisted for months on end as the Zimans' eviction applications languished at DHCR. In the meantime, the Zimans' tenants complained of harassment and reduction in services. Finally, after three hellish years of waiting, the Zimans finally received a decision: DHCR denied their eviction applications.

Having reached the point of no return, the Zimans challenged the decision in court. Reflecting back, Jerrold Ziman describes how they felt:

> Each step along the way, there was some other decision coming up that we thought might be in our favor. At some point, however, you realize you just lost your life. You don't find out you lost your life until about the third year into the deal. And then you're too far. Then you've done it. I don't know when we found out exactly that we lost our life. . . . It was so scary, so crazy.

Resigned to the battle, yet convinced that no matter what happened, he and his family would end up the losers, Jerrold Ziman recalls telling his wife Ellen that they had no future. "By the time we get this, our kids are going to be grown up. [Our lives will be] gone," he told her. When the Zimans had bought their home, their little girl was two, their boy seven. By the time they found their way to the end of the judicial gauntlet, their son was a teenager.

In addition to intangible losses, the battle was costly in monetary terms. The Zimans expended $100,000 to battle their way through two administrative proceedings and a trial court hearing, all of which yielded adverse rulings. Their ultimate costs would have been much higher were it not for the assistance provided by a pro-property rights group, the Competitive Enterprise Institute (CEI), which represented the Zimans in their proceedings with the intermediate and high courts of New York.

In those final proceedings, with the help of dedicated CEI attorney Sam Kazman, the Zimans finally won the courts' sympathy. The intermediate court ruled, and the high court affirmed, that the Zimans would be permitted to evict the tenants who occupied their home. To the disappointment of property-rights advocates, however, the grounds upon which the courts ruled in the Zimans' favor were narrow: the Zimans were found to be suffering a financial hardship owing to the small amount of income the property was generating, thereby qualifying them under a separate section of the law to evict their tenants. No judicial body ever found the anti-eviction law unconstitutional. In fact, no judicial body even recognized that the Zimans had a right to live in their house or to exclude others from so doing. Without such recognition, the most basic of property rights remains in jeopardy.

Lost in the bureaucratic tangle of rent regulations, the fight for the benefits of wealth redistribution, and the political power that comes from controlling it is the reality of rent control and what it does to people's lives. As Jerrold Ziman describes it,

> When you start getting your pockets picked, your property pulled right out of your pocket, and your life pulled right out of your heart, you know exactly where you're at. You feel it. You don't have to think about constitutional rights. You know that some tremendous, fundamental wrong has been done.

Local governments wreak havoc with people's property in other ways as well. One common scheme is to require property owners, as a condition for developing their property, to "contribute" to the public good in ways that have little or nothing to do with the owners' plans. Atlantic City, for example, passed an ordinance requiring builders to devote 1 percent of their construction budgets in projects costing more than $500,000 to the creation of works of art. As Thomas Carver, president of the Casino Association of New Jersey pointed out, "If it costs Donald Trump $1 billion to build the Taj Mahal, you can just imagine what the expense would be."[8]

The U.S. Supreme Court recently has exposed these forced payments for exactly what they are: extortion. In 1982, the Nollan family sought permission to replace their beachfront cottage with a larger home with enough room for their two children. The California Coastal Commission ruled that the Nollans could do so only if they ceded an easement to the state to allow unlimited public access to the beach.

The Nollans always had allowed public access, but wanted to preserve their right to exclude unruly people. But the coastal commission refused to back down. The result was a five-year legal battle in which Pacific Legal Foundation, representing the Nollans, took the case all the way to the U.S. Supreme Court. "The Coastal Commission historically has had an antagonistic and cavalier attitude toward property owners," explained James Patrick Nollan. "Had we been treated the least bit reasonably, maybe we would not be where we are today."[9]

The Supreme Court narrowly agreed with the Nollans, striking down the easement requirement as unconstitutional. Writing for the 5-4 majority, Justice Antonin Scalia declared that the commission's imposition of a condition unrelated to the permit application amounted to "an out-and-out plan of extortion."[10] The Court's stinging rebuke could force local governments to think twice before imposing on individual property owners the costs and burdens of societal do-gooding.

[8] Quoted in "Casinos Fighting Law Requiring Arts Gifts," *New York Times*, March 25, 1989.

[9] Kacy Sackett, "It's 'Champagne Time' at City Attorney's Beach House," *San Francisco Banner Daily Journal*, June 29, 1987, p. 6.

[10] *Nollan* v. *California Coastal Commission*, 483 U.S. 825, 837 (1987).

Another way in which local governments severely restrict property rights is through historic preservation ordinances. Under these laws, historic preservation commissions have the power to designate buildings as historical landmarks. Once a building is so designated, the ability of the owner to alter the building is curtailed, although the government pays nothing for the purported "public good" it thereby obtains.

The city of Pasadena's cultural heritage ordinance, for instance, encompasses buildings designed by certain architects as well as all those over 50 years old. Owners of such buildings must obtain the city's approval before demolishing or significantly altering the structures. The city can prevent the owners from tearing down or even painting the trim on such a building for more than a year, while the Cultural Heritage Commission tries to figure out ways to preserve the structure in its original form. Violators may be charged with a misdemeanor, forced to rebuild or restore the structure at their own cost, and prevented from obtaining a building permit for up to five years. Some officials had pushed for even heavier penalties: fines up to $1,000 per day for altering historical buildings without permission, and up to $50,000 for tearing down significant historical landmarks.[11]

The zoning and planning process itself often creates massive bureaucratic barriers that prevent individuals from using their property in ways they desire, without the government ever having to demonstrate that such barriers are necessary to protect the public.

An example of zoning from the 1940s has continuing ramifications today. Crystal Heights would have been Washington, D.C.'s only Frank Lloyd Wright creation, an enormous ornate structure consisting of 14 glass, bronze, and white marble towers of varying heights, to preside at the corner of Connecticut and Florida Avenues in the northwest quadrant of the city.[12] "It would have probably been Washington's best building," remarks Smithsonian Institution architectural historian Mina Marefat. "I certainly think it would have been Washington's most talked about building." Ironically, if it had been constructed, it surely would qualify today for historical

[11]Ashley Dunn, "Pasadena Moves to Save Old Buildings," *Los Angeles Times,* December 22, 1988.

[12]The following account is based primarily on William F. Powers, "Frank Lloyd Wright's Dream Deferred in District," *Washington Post,* July 4, 1992, pp. E1 and E4.

preservation protection. But the very same type of city planning bureaucrats who would seek to protect the building today prevented its construction 53 years ago. The opportunity to have what could have been Wright's supreme achievement was lost forever.

Wright's design was innovative in both form and function. "Basically, he was foreseeing the condo, yuppie lifestyle," explains Marefat. "He was suggesting . . . in 1940 a lifestyle that would provide the owner the opportunity to have hotel-like amenities, but an apartment they would own." Wright's Crystal Heights was to contain an art gallery, nine bowling lanes, a movie theater, retail shops, a cocktail lounge replete with 400-foot-long crystal bar, a banquet hall, and abundant underground parking. The towers would contain 2,500 apartments and hotel rooms.

Except for the necessary zoning variances, the project appeared to be a go. Architect Wright and his developer, Roy S. Thurman, had the site, plans, and funding. But the District Zoning Commission effectively prevented development of Crystal Heights. For starters, one of the project's towers exceeded the District's building height restriction by 25 feet. The commission denied the necessary variances, and the project was halted. As a result of the city planners' zeal to protect Washingtonians from an extra 25 feet of glass, bronze, and marble, the project is forever the unrealized and now unrealizable idea of a man recognized as perhaps America's premier architectural genius.

If Frank Lloyd Wright could not win approval for Crystal Heights, imagine the obstacles ordinary property owners encounter when they try to develop their property in ways that offend the tastes or sensitivities of planning bureaucrats. The time and expense involved in red tape are tremendous, and decisions are costly and difficult to challenge. Although the courts generally are now more vigilant about requiring compensation for takings of property, local governments often circumvent these limits by tying up property owners in endless bureaucratic red tape until the owners give up, give in, or run out of money. Meanwhile, the innumerable government officials who make up the countless boards and commissions remain largely invisible and unaccountable to the public whose rights they regulate.

Most Americans cherish property. Those who don't own property aspire to do so. Recognizing this fact, bipartisan legislation sponsored by Rep. Jack Kemp was enacted during the Reagan administration, providing opportunities for low-income residents of public housing to manage and eventually own their dwellings. Even here, the battle lines over property rights are drawn between individuals and local governments: public housing authorities around the country engage in tactics ranging from bribery to retaliation in a frenzied effort to safeguard their fiefdoms.[13] The battle over tenant management and ownership of public housing reveals grassroots tyranny in an especially ugly form, for it pits powerful unelected bureaucrats against disadvantaged people trying to gain control over their destinies.

Property gives individuals an ownership stake in the American dream. But despite clear constitutional protection for property rights, Americans have precious little recourse against overzealous government regulators. Excessive property regulations add tens of thousands of dollars to the cost of housing construction, preventing economic outsiders from obtaining homeownership or moving to better communities. Meanwhile, those who own property have no assurance they can develop it or that government won't take it.

In a system that respects property rights, the government should have the burden of justifying infringements of those rights. A limit of this nature is compelled both by the requirement of the Fifth Amendment that takings of property must be for "public use," as well as the Fourteenth Amendment's prohibition against depriving people of property without due process of law.

This rule would have several important ramifications. As a threshold matter, any time a government takes property, it must demonstrate that its action is taken to further a public purpose. Where it limits the use of property, it should show that its regulation is necessary to further legitimate government objectives. Finally, when the owner is deprived of substantial use or enjoyment of property, even by regulation, the government should provide reasonable compensation for the property rights taken.

Such modest restrictions would leave intact government power to protect public health and safety, but would also greatly inhibit excessive, unnecessary, or capricious government regulation. And they would go far in strengthening one of the essential pillars of freedom in our society.

[13]"Kemp Seeks Investigation of Housing Agencies," *Washington Post*, July 17, 1992.

7. Freedom of Speech

They arrived at the art gallery on a Saturday morning in April 1990. They weren't dressed in the secret police uniforms befitting their mission, but instead wore ordinary business attire, mingling freely with the hundreds of patrons attending the show. "I'm only here to view the exhibit," declared one of them.[1]

But that was not all that the anonymous sleuths had in mind, for, as sheriff's officers and local grand jury members, they had come to inspect the objects on display at the Cincinnati Contemporary Arts Center so that they could determine whether any of them were obscene. Ironically, these agents of morality became a spectacle themselves, their presence evoking attention from gallery officials and news reporters. Taking in the scene, gallery director Dennis Barrie remarked, "God, it's hard to tell who's press, who's vice, [and] who's a paying customer."

The exhibit everyone was there to see was a collection of 175 photographs by the late Robert Mapplethorpe. The principal subjects of the photographs were flowers and nude people. The nudes included homoerotic photos and portraits of children taken with their parents' permission.

Most of the people in attendance were merely enjoying the exhibition, but the officials who had been dispatched by the local government had a different objective: to shut it down. The investigation team was seeking evidence sufficient to brand some of the photos "obscene," which would provide the basis for a court order closing the show.

That afternoon, the Cincinnati grand jury concluded that seven of the photos were obscene and issued indictments in Hamilton County court against Barrie and the arts center on two criminal misdemeanor counts of pandering obscenity and illegal use of a

[1]The following account is based primarily on Kim Masters, "Police Ordered to Let Photo Exhibit Go On," *Washington Post*, April 9, 1990, p. C1; and Judy Keen, "Case Could Reverberate Across USA," *USA Today*, September 24, 1990, p. 1A.

minor in nudity-oriented material. If convicted, the arts center would be liable for up to $10,000 in fines, and Barrie could be fined an additional $2,000 and sentenced to as much as six months in jail.

County prosecutor Arthur Ney called a 2:30 p.m. news conference to announce the indictments. Minutes later, more than a dozen sheriff's deputies and police officers moved in, ordering more than 450 visitors and reporters to leave the arts center while they videotaped the exhibition. No photographs were seized, but Sheriff Simon Leis warned of additional legal action against the gallery and its board members if the targeted photos were not removed.

Instead, the center's lawyers countered with an action against the local authorities. Within a few days, Judge Carl Rubin granted an injunction against the city officials. "You may not remove any photographs," Rubin instructed the authorities. "You may not close the exhibit to the public. You may not take any action which would be intimidating in nature to prevent the public from seeing this exhibit." Judge Rubin acknowledged that the exhibit had aroused strong emotion in the community, as it had in other cities. Nonetheless, he instructed that "I want it clearly understood . . . [that] the notion of crowd control, which may be necessary, may not be used as an excuse to close down this exhibit."

The judge's ruling gave Dennis Barrie and the arts center a temporary reprieve, but not a complete victory. Barrie would still have to stand trial in state court, and Rubin ordered the gallery to provide county prosecutors with exact duplicates of the targeted pictures. Meanwhile, county prosecutors refused to back off, warning the gallery that police officers "certainly can return on a daily basis" to determine whether the exhibition had been altered in any way.

Four months after the exhibition left town, and more than five months after police raided the gallery, Barrie and the arts center were tried on the criminal charges before a jury selected from the community. The lawsuit attracted national attention, for its implications went far beyond the individuals involved. As Barrie declared, "What's at stake here are fundamental freedoms—freedom of expression and the access to that freedom."

The concept of free speech encompasses not only the individual's right to speak—to express one's self through art, political tracts, or even flag burning—but also the right of others to judge for thcmselves whether or not to listen or see. The constant struggle between freedom of expression and efforts to suppress it is one whose outcome reflects whether a society is free or unfree.

The Mapplethorpe controversy illustrated vividly the interplay between free expression and the forces of suppression. The exhibition at the heart of the controversy exemplified the voluntarism that lies at the core of free speech: no one was forced to visit the show or to like it if they did. It was open to the public to patronize or not, as each individual freely might choose.

But for Monty Lobb of the 16,000-member Citizens for Community Values, "The real issue is that people realize they're raising their children in a society with a corrupting influence." The fact that the gallery prohibited children under 18 (even infants in their parents' arms) from viewing the exhibit made no difference to the citizens committee. Nor did it matter that Mapplethorpe was a globally renowned artist whose photographs of flowers would elicit gasps of appreciation from even the most conservative ladies' floral society, or that no public funds supported the exhibition. None of these things mattered because the citizens committee had installed itself as the moral arbiter for the entire community, and it was offended by the mere presence of the exhibition in Cincinnati. On that basis, the committee was quite willing to use the coercive power of government to rid the city of the perceived evil—to substitute its collective moral judgment for the voluntary decisions of individual citizens. In a very real sense, then, not only were Barrie and the arts center on trial, but the First Amendment and America's commitment to freedom of speech were on trial as well.

Fortunately for believers in artistic freedom, the jury ultimately found Barrie and the arts center not guilty. But the fact that the gallery and its officials had to go to court twice—once to stop police officers from seizing privately owned photographs, and again to defend themselves against criminal charges for exhibiting the photographs—sent shock waves across the nation. As civil liberties columnist Nat Hentoff predicted, even if the effort in Cincinnati to suppress the Mapplethorpe exhibition failed, "there are museum directors elsewhere—reckoning the cost of an obscenity defense— who may well be more cautious from now on."[2] Self-censorship

---

[2]Nat Hentoff, "Is There Anything Left to Ban in Cincinnati?" *Washington Post*, August 4, 1990, p. A23.

based upon fear of prosecution is potentially as effective a means of suppression as outright censorship.

The specter of police storming art galleries to seize purportedly offensive art conjures images of Nazi Germany, where the government raided museums and expropriated thousands of paintings, sculptures, and graphics it deemed "degenerate."[3] The impulse to say "it can't happen here" is offset by the constant efforts throughout America today, from both ends of the political spectrum, to suppress speech deemed offensive by whatever faction controls the levers of government. From the banning of Bibles in public schools to the banning of classics such as *Huckleberry Finn* on the grounds that they stereotype minorities, from the censorship of rock lyrics to the suppression of politically incorrect speech on college campuses, America's cherished tradition of free speech is perhaps in graver jeopardy today than at any time since the Alien and Sedition Acts.

The Framers of the Bill of Rights recognized the primary importance of free speech in ensuring a free society, and they made its protection first among the Constitution's enumerated liberties. They understood that the best way to counteract unpopular or offensive speech was not by suppressing it but by more speech, and they appreciated that the greatest threat to free speech was the power of government.

Hence, the First Amendment established the only absolute guarantee of a free market in the Constitution: the free marketplace of ideas. The command is simple and unequivocal: "Congress shall make no law . . . abridging the freedom of speech, or of the press." This limit on government power was extended to the states and localities through the Fourteenth Amendment.

The courts have long recognized that freedom of speech is not absolute. The government may adopt reasonable and nondiscriminatory regulations of the time, place, and manner in which free speech is exercised. It may limit the access of minors to certain types of speech. It may punish speakers who engage in illegal conduct, such as trespass. What is absolutely sacrosanct under the First Amendment, however, is the content of speech, which is off-limits to government suppression.

[3]Robert Darnton, "Fall of the House of Art," *New Republic*, May 6, 1991, p. 27.

Yet, the contemporary trend is to suppress speech precisely because of its content, particularly by using the coercive power of government at the state and local levels. The courts have fueled this phenomenon in several areas. For instance, in the areas of obscenity and pornography—which are not considered "speech" by the courts and are therefore unprotected by the First Amendment—the courts apply a subjective community standard to determine whether or not speech is obscene and hence whether the government may suppress it. In its 1973 decision in *Miller* v. *California*, the Supreme Court set forth a three-part test for determining whether a particular work is obscene:

(1) Would the average person, applying contemporary community standards, find that the work, taken as a whole, appeals to the "prurient interest"?
(2) Does the work describe or depict, in a patently offensive way, sexual conduct specifically defined by the applicable state obscenity law?
(3) Does the work, taken as a whole, lack serious literary, artistic, political, or scientific value?[4]

The *Miller* decision seriously weakened the protections of the First Amendment. Freedom of speech would cease to be uniform: it would vary from place to place, in accordance with the standards of each particular community and the provisions of state laws. Although the First Amendment was designed to operate as a universal prohibition against government censorship, its protections were now made dependent upon the standards of the would-be censors themselves, creating enormous potential for grassroots tyranny.

Fortunately, the Supreme Court ruled in 1987 that the third part of the *Miller* test—whether the work has serious literary, artistic, political, or scientific value—would be determined not by reference to community standards but in accordance with a "reasonable person" standard.[5] But again, the Court's test inevitably will substitute a particular value judgment whether of a judge, state legislature, jury, or community—for the judgment the First Amendment

[4]*Miller* v. *California*, 413 U.S. 15 (1973).
[5]*Pope* v. *Illinois*, 481 U.S. 497 (1987).

entrusts to each and every individual. This distinction has enormous real-world ramifications: in the realm of speech or expression today, where an individual's judgment strays from that of the community—or of the judicially determined reasonable person—criminal penalties may follow, even if the conduct involved is voluntary and harms no one. We have journeyed far from the free marketplace of ideas that is the bedrock of our American republic.

Moreover, controversial art is not the only thing at stake in the censorship war. Government-sanctioned intolerance threatens the very essence of our humanness as expressed through personality, personal association, and lifestyle.[6] Ask Robert George, whose own Glendale, California, city government in November 1987 obtained an injunction against him declaring that "No member of the public may enter or remain on [his] property," except relatives and "bona fide personal friends [or] public employees, deliverymen and/or public utility personnel," and prohibiting George's "distribution of business cards, documents or other information" advertising his address. What crime did George commit to warrant such a harsh response? He impersonates Santa Claus, opening his festive, heavily decorated home to disabled and terminally ill children who wish to spend a little time with Saint Nick.

Neighbors complained to the Glendale city government, first alleging that George was operating a business in a residential zone and then that George had created a public nuisance by drawing traffic to the area. One neighbor wrote a letter to the local newspaper protesting that George's "rented home is . . . nothing special and actually looks cheap," and that the neighbors have their "dignity to uphold." Another neighbor complained that Santa's guests were subjecting neighbors to "verbal abuse." She protested: "We are being openly criticized for watering our lawns, for not having sidewalks, and for daring to express our concerns." In addition,

[6]Carolyn Jacobson, "Peace, Quiet and Tranquility for Alameda Avenue" (letter to the editor), *Glendale News-Press*, December 27, 1986, p. A-4; "Bah! Humbug! Ex-Nebraskan Meets Scrooge," *Omaha World-Herald*, November 27, 1987, p. 17; John Ordaz, "Glendale Santa Should Be Declared Public Nuisance" (letter to the editor), *Glendale News-Press*, November 30, 1987; James Christopher, "Reader Says City Has Been Fooled by Santa Claus" (letter to the editor), *Glendale News-Press*, December 9, 1987; Doug Smith, "It's Christmas in March for Glendale's Resident Santa," *Los Angeles Times*, March 30, 1989, part II, p. 3; and *City of Glendale* v. *George*, slip op., no. BO32383 (Cal. App. Second App. Dist., March 27, 1989).

she argued that the Santa operation created a real potential for crime. "A man was nearly beaten to death early Sunday night while walking his dog on Alameda Avenue . . . one-half block from Santa's Circus," she pointed out. A third resident said the "neighbors simply don't want [Santa] on their block anymore," and suggested that George, who is the son of Lebanese immigrants, move to Beirut.

In response to these gripes, the city of Glendale went after Santa Claus, alleging in a complaint to the court that he had created a public nuisance. In November 1987, George and the city agreed to a consent judgment and permanent injunction, which prohibited him from advertising his address and characterizing it, publicly or privately, as the residence of Santa Claus; limited visitors to George's home; and restricted his use of lights and ornaments, among other constraints. George regretted entering into the agreement, and says he was pushed into it. "If I [didn't] sign . . . they [were going to] come in here and take me to jail," he explained.

Shortly after making the agreement, George moved to have it set aside and vacated on the grounds that it violated his First Amendment rights of expression and association. He was unsuccessful in the superior court, but in March 1989, with the help of the American Civil Liberties Union (ACLU), he prevailed in the court of appeals. Although restrictions on George's use of Christmas decorations were left intact, the provisions of the agreement limiting George's visitors and ability to represent his home as that of Santa and give out his address were struck down as violative of the First Amendment.

Without the pressure created by media coverage, the legal muscle lent by the ACLU, and an 18-month court battle, George might still be living under the constraints placed upon him by the city of Glendale. But not every victim of grassroots tyranny is as fortunate as he. Many do not have the resources to fight the government. And with courts increasingly reluctant to rule in favor of First Amendment liberties, many may find there exists little recourse against overly zealous local governments.

The erosion of freedom of speech manifests itself in numerous ways that affect our daily lives. Art galleries and eccentrics are not the only ones feeling the heat of suppression these days. Supermarkets and real estate businesses are equally susceptible to government censorship; indeed, in light of recent court decisions, they may have even less First Amendment protection than adult bookstores. At least that's what Rep. David Mann, formerly a Cincinnati city council member, hopes.

While on the city council, Mann was offended at the proliferation of news racks on the public streets. "We were being overwhelmed by ugly boxes," Mann explained. "Ugly blue. Ugly green. Ugly red." So he decided to do something about it. The city couldn't ban the dissemination of all newspapers on the streets, so instead it banned only newsracks offering purely commercial publications: real estate guides, brochures for educational and recreational services, and other consumer information. Despite the fact that only 62 of the city's 2,000 newsracks carried such publications—and that ordinary newspapers themselves contain large amounts of commercial advertising—the city felt justified in adopting the discriminatory ban. "I love it," gloated Mann. "The boxes were garish. But it was more than aesthetic. Why should purely advertising materials have a right to be on our street? Soon Proctor & Gamble would want to put out coupons for Ivory Soap." The citizens of Cincinnati must consider themselves fortunate to have their elected officials so diligently protecting them from such horrible fates.[7]

That Cincinnati could consider so crudely stifling the free flow of commercial information is the result of a peculiar interpretation of the First Amendment. In the realm of commercial speech—that is, any speech that proposes a commercial transaction—the Supreme Court has virtually eliminated constitutional protection against state regulation or control. The Court has redrafted the First Amendment to read, in effect, that government "shall make no law . . . abridging the freedom of speech—except commercial speech, which government may abridge with impunity."

The Supreme Court's commercial speech doctrine represents its starkest renunciation of the absolute and unequivocal terms of the First Amendment. Indeed, among all types of speech, commercial speech is singled out for nonprotection by the courts despite the fact, as the Supreme Court has recognized, that the ordinary citizen's interest in commercial information is "as keen, if not keener by far, than his interest in the day's most urgent public debate."[8]

[7]Joan Biskupic, "Handbill Law Is First Amendment Test," *Washington Post,* November 8, 1992, p. A8.

[8]*Virginia State Board of Pharmacy* v. *Virginia Citizens Consumer Council,* 425 U.S. 748, 763 (1976).

Thc Supreme Court first established a commercial speech doctrine in a 1942 decision upholding a ban against distribution of any
"handbill [or] other advertising matter [in] or upon any street."[9]
Although noting that a similar ban on other types of expression
would violate the First Amendment, the Court ruled that there is
"no such restraint on government as respects purely commercial
advertising."[10] The Court made no attempt to justify the distinction
between noncommercial speech, which received extensive First
Amendment protection, and commercial speech, which received
none at all.[11]

The judicial renunciation of free commercial speech lasted until
1972, when a group of consumers challenged in the U.S. Supreme
Court a Virginia law that prohibited any advertising of prescription
drug prices. The state defended the ban on the grounds that advertising might induce consumers to patronize low-cost, low-quality
pharmacies and therefore drive professional pharmacists out of
business and lower professional standards. As the Court summarized the state's argument, "All this can be avoided if [consumers]
are not permitted to know who is charging what."[12]

In a ringing triumph for freedom of speech, the Court struck
down the ban. Writing for the majority, Justice Harry Blackmun
declared,

> There is, of course, an alternative to this highly paternalis-
> tic approach. That alternative is to assume that this informa-
> tion is not in itself harmful, that people will perceive their
> own best interests if only they are well enough informed,
> and that the best means to that end is to open the channels
> of communication rather than to close them. . . . But the
> choice among these alternatives is not ours to make or the
> Virginia General Assembly's. It is precisely this kind of
> choice, between the dangers of suppressing information,
> and the dangers of its misuse if it is freely available, that
> the First Amendment makes for us.[13]

[9]*Valentine* v. *Chrestensen*, 316 U.S. 52 (1942).

[10]Ibid.

[11]Ibid.

[12]*Virginia Pharmacy*, p. 770.

[13]*Virginia Pharmacy*, pp. 76–77. This decision is also important because it recognized
that not only speakers but also consumers of speech have legal standing to challenge
government restrictions on the free flow of speech.

The Court cautioned that the First Amendment's protection of commercial speech is not absolute. It does not forbid reasonable regulation of advertising, nor does it extend to false or misleading speech or to speech about illegal transactions. But the Court's decision in *Virginia Pharmacy* extended First Amendment protection to an entire realm of speech that was previously excluded.

The sunshine cast upon commercial speech didn't last long, however. Indeed, the dark cloud of the Court's future retrenchment on commercial speech appeared on the horizon in Justice William Rehnquist's dissent in *Virginia Pharmacy*. Although the majority's decision might represent "desirable public policy," Rehnquist quipped, "there is certainly nothing in the United States Constitution which requires the Virginia Legislature to hew to the teachings of Adam Smith in its legislative decisions regulating the pharmacy profession."[14] Rehnquist apparently would exorcise the free market from the free marketplace of ideas that the First Amendment was designed to protect.

By the late 1980s, a majority of the Court began to heed Rehnquist's call to once again banish commercial speech to jurisprudential purgatory. In the 1986 *Posadas* case, the Court upheld a ban on advertising of legal casino gambling imposed by the government of Puerto Rico.[15] The advertising did not fall into any of the areas that the *Virginia Pharmacy* decision recognized as justifying restrictions on commercial speech. The advertising was neither fraudulent nor deceptive, and the activity involved is lawful in Puerto Rico. Nonetheless, the Court, with Chief Justice Rehnquist now commanding a majority, announced a sweeping new exception to First Amendment protection for commercial speech. Acknowledging that the Court previously had struck down bans on advertising of contraceptives and abortion clinics, Rehnquist explained that in those cases "the subject of the advertising restrictions was constitutionally protected and could not have been prohibited by the State."[16] But in this case, Rehnquist observed, the legislature "surely could have prohibited casino gambling by the residents of

---

[14]Ibid., at 784 (Rehnquist, J., dissenting).

[15]*Posadas de Puerto Rico Associates* v. *Tourism Company of Puerto Rico*, 478 U.S. 328, 345–46 (1986).

[16]Ibid.

Puerto Rico altogether."[17] This "greater power to completely ban casino gambling," Rehnquist reasoned, "necessarily includes the lesser power to ban advertising."[18]

The *Posadas* doctrine could mean the virtual elimination of constitutional protection for commercial speech, for the courts have imposed few limits on the power of state and local governments to ban or regulate economic activities (see chapter 8). Indeed, abortion and contraceptives may be the only commercial activities that have received constitutional protection. Taken to its logical extreme, *Posadas* could unleash cities and states to ban everything from "for sale" signs to Girl Scouts selling cookies.

Dissenting in *Posadas*, Justice William Brennan expressed serious concern over the new rationale for censorship embraced by the majority. The First Amendment, Brennan declared, dictates that government

> may not suppress the dissemination of truthful information about entirely lawful activity merely to keep its residents ignorant. The Court, however, would allow Puerto Rico to do just that, thus dramatically shrinking the scope of First Amendment protection available to commercial speech, and giving government officials unprecedented authority to eviscerate constitutionally protected expression.[19]

Business owner Mary Lynn Rasmussen learned firsthand about her government's zeal to regulate commercial speech, when she was denied permission in 1991 to advertise her Okie Girl Restaurant on a sign at a freeway offramp.[20] The California Department of Transportation (Caltrans) objected not to any activity conducted at the restaurant, but to its very name. "Okie," it decided, was a "slanderous slur" on Oklahomans, and Caltrans had a duty to protect motorists from such offensive language.

Apparently Rasmussen's status as a native Oklahoman was of no consequence to the self-appointed experts on matters offensive to Oklahomans. Ironically, after prohibiting the ad, Caltrans did hear from hundreds of Oklahomans, including Gov. David Walters.

[17]Ibid.

[18]Ibid.

[19]Ibid., at 358–59 (Brennan, J., dissenting).

[20]Charles Oliver, "Brickbats," *Reason* (July 1991), p. 18.

Those people were indeed offended, not by the use of the word "Okie", but by Caltrans' characterization of it as offensive! They liked to call themselves Okies and thought Ms. Rasmussen ought to be able to call herself one too.

Having heard from enough Okies, Caltrans agreed to permit the Okie Girl Restaurant to advertise by its name. Not satisfied, however, to relinquish control over the characterization of Oklahomans in advertising, it then prohibited Rasmussen from using her logo. The logo, which depicts a buxom country girl wearing a straw hat and cutoff overalls, was deemed "offensive to good taste and decency."

Fed up, Rasmussen hired a lawyer and challenged the prohibition. She eventually succeeded in obtaining a settlement allowing her to use her logo and awarding her $32,500. Perhaps the next time Caltrans sets out to protect the sensibilities of motorists, it will stop to consider the sensibilities of taxpayers, who must foot the bill for its caprice.

Government-sponsored thought control and ignorance, enforced through the suppression of speech, is by no means restricted to the commercial arena. Indeed, the drive to invest the state with the power to dictate the boundaries of permissible speech has moved to the one institution traditionally committed above all others to the free exchange of ideas: the university.

For the sake of political correctness, a new intellectual elite is demanding ideological orthodoxy on college campuses, and is seeking to enforce it through censorship. This phenomenon illustrates that the suppression of speech is not at all the exclusive province of moral majoritarians; rather, it is a weapon readily wielded by zealots at either end of the spectrum.

The means to achieve these ends, as ACLU president Nadine Strossen has observed, are "speech codes that restrict what students can say on the basis of content."[21] From coast to coast, colleges and universities—including public universities, which are subject to the First Amendment—have adopted codes banning such evils as "intolerance," "stigmatiz[ing]" conduct, and "certain types of

---

[21]See "Politically Correct Speech and the First Amendment," *Cato Policy Report* (March/April 1991), pp. 6–7.

134

expressive behavior directed at individuals," with penalties ranging from written warnings to expulsion.[22]

The speech codes are designed to restrict racist, sexist, homophobic, or otherwise offensive speech. Defenders of the codes, Strossen observes, invoke "noble goals that, considered in their own right, nobody could quarrel with. Who's in favor of sexual harassment? Who's in favor of undermining equality of educational opportunity on the basis of sex and race?" But however worthy the goals, Strossen notes, people are now starting to recognize "the adverse impact on free speech of attempts to attain these goals by imposing speech codes." Viewed in the broader context of the drive to promote "political correctness" on college campuses, Strossen warns that the speech codes reflect an attempt to dictate "what you must say, what you must think, what you must teach, and what you must study."

However well-intentioned, the speech codes produce the same consequences as all other types of suppression of speech. In a sense, they may achieve an effect that is precisely the opposite of their intent, for although speech can be regulated or suppressed, thoughts can not be. And if speech is suppressed, thoughts may be expressed in ways that are much more harmful than spoken words. Moreover, once the notion is validated that speech can be censored if it is "offensive," enormous discretion is vested in whoever gives meaning to that vague term. In the early days of the republic, President Andrew Jackson proposed banning the distribution of "inflammatory" antislavery publications in much the same way as today's censors seek to ban speech they find offensive.[23] Nadine Strossen aptly describes what is at stake: "I thought it was clearly understood that the central principle of the Bill of Rights is the indivisibility of rights. . . . [I]f any person or any group is deprived of any right, then all rights are endangered for all people and all groups."

But perhaps the gravest consequence is the chilling effect that the codes have on the free exchange of ideas that is the hallmark of a university and at the core of the First Amendment's guarantees.

[22]See, for example, Chester E. Finn, Jr., "An Island of Repression in a Sea of Freedom," *Commentary* (September 1989), p. 17.

[23]Clint Bolick, *Changing Course: Civil Rights at the Crossroads* (New Brunswick, N.J.: Transaction Books, 1988), pp. 19–20.

If words are forbidden if they fall into vague and subjective categories such as "offensive," "hostile," or "intimidating," people will likely steer clear of such nebulous boundaries and refrain from engaging in the exchange of ideas, particularly if their academic standing is at risk.

One victim of the new censorship on college campuses was James Taranto, at the time a journalism student at California State University at Northridge (CSUN), who worked as a news editor at the campus newspaper, the *Daily Sundial*.[24] Taranto was suspended from the newspaper's staff for two weeks without pay for writing about "controversial matters" without the faculty adviser's permission. Of course, controversial matters are the life blood of most newspapers, but in this instance the issue discussed was not only controversial but also, in the eyes of the university's censors, politically incorrect. Taranto paid the price.

The incident that triggered Taranto's suspension actually traced its origins to an earlier episode at the University of California at Los Angeles (UCLA). Ron Bell, editor of the UCLA student paper, printed a cartoon depicting a character known as the U.C. rooster. In the comic strip, a person notices the bird and remarks, "Wow, that's cool, but how did you get into UCLA?" To which the rooster replies, "Affirmative action."

Bell was suspended from his position as editor for violating a rule prohibiting "articles that perpetuate derogatory ethnic or cultural stereotypes." Bell's crime was ridiculing affirmative action. As it was later explained to Taranto by his own faculty adviser, the cartoon, "though it mentioned no ethnic group, was a violation of the UCLA rule because affirmative action applies only to women and minorities." Bell was reinstated after publishing an apology.[25]

Taranto took to Bell's defense in an editorial in the *Daily Sundial* that blasted the censorship at UCLA and reproduced the rooster cartoon, whereupon he promptly was suspended from the staff for violating the rule against pre-clearance of controversial material. Unlike Bell, however, Taranto declined to apologize for exercising

[24]Taranto also noted that an article in the black UCLA student newspaper attacking the character of whites was not similarly censored because "white people are neither an ethnic nor a cultural group." James Taranto, "No Longer Teaching Tolerance," *Orange County Register*, June 19, 1988.

[25]"The Rooster Papers," *The Quill* (September 1988), pp. 16–22.

his First Amendment rights, and instead filed a lawsuit with the help of the ACLU. Before long, the university backed down and settled the lawsuit, agreeing to give Taranto $93 in back pay and to remove the suspension from his academic record. More importantly, the university altered its policy, allowing faculty review only in cases of potential libel, invasion of privacy, or obscenity. Thanks to Taranto's bold stand, the school's policy now states, "Students working on the Sundial are fully protected by the First Amendment of the Constitution from censorship by the faculty, school administration, and state officials." Taranto's news conference announcing the university's capitulation was attended by former attorney general Edwin Meese and the ACLU's Morton Halperin, whose joint presence demonstrated the breadth of support for free speech on college campuses.[26]

Although Taranto's story had a happy ending, the traditional commitment to the free exchange of ideas on college campuses continues to erode. Revealing the Orwellian nature of speech codes, CSUN journalism department chairman Michael Emery objected to the ACLU's lawsuit on behalf of Taranto, complaining, "What about the possibility the American Civil Liberties Union has, by filing suit, unwittingly assisted in an attack on . . . academic freedom?"[27] The disturbing notion that "academic freedom" means the freedom to suppress ideas illustrates vividly the transformation of universities from citadels of learning to bastions of political correctness. In the name of diversity, the speech codes produce exactly the opposite result, threatening to turn the campus, in the words of civil rights scholar Abigail Thernstrom, into "an island of repression in a sea of freedom."[28]

The propensity of government to censor speech grows all the more ominous with the development of new communications technologies that frequently are subject to government control. Government regulation of most of the new communications technologies is exercised primarily at the national level. The principal exception, however, is a vitally important one: cable television. Over half

---

[26]Carol Innerst, "ACLU, Meese Condemn Colleges' Anti-conservatism," *Washington Times*, May 17, 1989, p. A1.

[27]"The Rooster Papers," p. 22.

[28]Quoted in Finn, p. 23.

the nation's households are subscribers, giving local governments, which possess wide-ranging regulatory authority over cable television, tremendous influence over the flow of information in today's society.

Imagine a city government deciding to exercise control over the local daily newspaper. The government reasons that the distribution of the newspaper on city streets furnishes a justification to regulate the paper. Moreover, because economic forces have reduced newspaper competition, the government decides it needs to regulate the newspaper in the interest of its residents. So it invites bids to win the right for the newspaper franchise. The bidding process requires would-be newspaper publishers to wine and dine public officials, to pay huge franchise fees to the city, and to engage in other activities that are little short of outright bribery. The government gives itself the power to oversee the content of the newspaper, and requires the paper to turn over several pages for the use of the local government and special-interest groups. In return, the government confers a monopoly upon the winning competitor, prohibiting competition from all other newspapers.

Such a scenario would be blatantly unconstitutional if a city government ever tried it in the context of newspapers, but that is precisely the scenario that has played out in virtually every city in America in the context of cable television. Yet, the rationale for local government control of cable television is no greater than it is for newspapers, and the implications are certainly no less ominous.

In 99.5 percent of cities that have cable, the service is provided on a monopoly basis, despite the fact that competition is readily available from other nearby cable companies and from competing communications technologies. As *Consumers Research* editor John Merline has charged, "Cable monopolies are *created* monopolies—resulting not from natural economic forces but from burdensome regulations imposed by city governments."[29]

The process of awarding the exclusive franchise essentially shifts the competition from the marketplace to the political realm. As a result, cable television companies tailor their pitch not to consumers (who have no choice except to patronize the monopoly company

[29]John Merline, "Tuning out Cable TV Monopolies," *Washington Post*, May 19, 1991, pp. D1, D5 (emphasis in original).

138

chosen by the government) but to politicians. The consequences are predictable: lots of giveaways to the politicians (such as televising of city council meetings, studios for special-interest group programming, minority set-asides, hefty franchise fees, etc.), and high prices and poor service for the consumers. Federal legislation in the mid-1980s removed from localities the power to control prices, resulting in a largely unregulated government-conferred monopoly. Exorbitant prices predictably followed, leading Congress in 1992 to restore rate controls. Cable television now is a full-fledged government monopoly like electric utilities, despite the important role it plays in the dissemination of speech in contemporary society.

In the handful of cities where competition exists, consumers benefit. In the period between 1986 and 1989, the Storer Communications cable monopoly in Montgomery, Alabama, imposed steep price increases every year without expanding service. But in 1990, a competing cable company started laying cables in the city. The result? Storer upgraded its basic service to 61 channels and cut its price by almost two dollars a month. A survey of 52 markets found that cable companies in cities with competition offer more channels at a considerably lower price than cities with cable monopolies, with monopoly companies charging 30 percent more per channel. The pervasive system of government-imposed cable monopolies thus has the effect of substantially increasing the cost of receiving communications.[30]

To make matters worse, the huge monopoly windfalls produced by the cable television franchise process play into the propensity toward corruption in local governments. As economist Thomas Hazlett has reported, the "sleaziness of cable TV—ranging from palm greasing in exchange for franchise rights to the steep rate hikes that an unregulated monopoly can impose"—reflects the "shady symbiosis between politicians and cable TV franchises found all across the country."[31]

What all this means is that the source from which millions of Americans receive much of their news, consumer information, and entertainment is controlled by local government to a degree never

[30]Ibid.
[31]Thomas Hazlett, "Wired," *New Republic*, May 29, 1989, p. 11.

before tolerated under the First Amendment. It means that consumers are offered (and pay for whether they want to or not) such shows as "The Governor Meets the Press" and "The Florida League of Cities." But they can't choose among cable companies or otherwise enjoy the benefits of competition. It also means that the content of cable television is controlled, to a large degree, by whoever controls the levers of power in city hall. The power of local government to control cable television has not yet been determined by the courts. How this question is resolved may ultimately determine the future vitality of free speech in America.

The relationship between local government and freedom of speech has always been an uneasy one, and suppression of speech is one of the most common and pernicious forms of grassroots tyranny. Traditionally, the courts have stepped in to curb excesses, striking down various forms of local government censorship of speech, ranging from door-to-door religious solicitations to civil rights demonstrations to flag burning to theatrical productions. But such protection of this vital freedom is no longer assured, as the Supreme Court expends evermore energy on finding exceptions to freedom of speech rather than protecting that freedom.

As a result, advocates of liberty must devote their own energy to demonstrating the seminal importance of freedom of speech in a free society. That freedom is not without limits: government has a wide latitude under the First Amendment to maintain public order and to protect the fundamental rights of all its citizens. But all too often, government strays beyond its proper role by curtailing expression merely because it finds it offensive or unpopular.

The examples in this chapter, as well as many others throughout American history, demonstrate that the impulse toward suppression is not unique to a particular ideology. Whoever has the power to censor today may have his or her ideas censored tomorrow. Only by adhering to the absolute protection of freedom of speech set forth in the First Amendment—only by protecting the freedom of speech of every one of us—can we protect the freedom of speech of any of us. And only by holding local governments to that principle can we avoid grassroots tyranny that manifests itself in the suppression of the free marketplace of ideas.

8. Economic Liberty

The little business owned and operated by Taalib-Din Abdul Uqdah and his wife, Pamela Ferrell, is a classic American success story.[1] Uqdah and Ferrell launched Cornrows & Co. in northwest Washington, D.C., with a little capital and lots of skill and savvy. A decade later, the business was grossing half a million dollars a year and providing beautiful and intricate braided hairstyles for thousands of satisfied customers.

If Uqdah and Ferrell did well, they also did good. In times of high unemployment and fiscal shortfalls in the District of Columbia, Cornrows & Co. contributed more than its share to the welfare of the community. In addition to paying tens of thousands of dollars in annual local taxes and establishing a national toll-free hair-care hotline, Cornrows & Co. trained and hired dozens of previously unemployed and unskilled individuals, many of whom went on to start their own businesses.

In 1992, Cornrows & Co. celebrated its twelfth year in the hair-braiding business. In January of that year, the District of Columbia dispatched an emissary bearing a special new year's greeting from the government: a summons ordering Uqdah to shut down his business immediately or go to jail.

The summons was the culmination of a battle between Uqdah and the District government that had raged since soon after Cornrows & Co. had opened its doors. The city was not concerned about health and safety problems. After 12 years of operation and regular inspections by District officials, Cornrows & Co. never had been cited for a single health or safety violation or consumer complaint. Rather, what concerned the city was Cornrows & Co.'s failure to obtain licenses from the District of Columbia Board of Cosmetology.

Under a law dating back to 1938, every person employed by a "beauty shop" in Washington, D.C., must obtain an "operator's"

[1]The following account is based primarily on the author's personal knowledge as attorney for Uqdah and Ferrell.

license. To do so, an individual must take an 11-month course at an approved cosmetology school at a cost of up to $5,000. Graduates then must pass an examination administered by the cosmetology board, consisting of written and performance components. The test requires demonstrated proficiency in hairstyles that haven't been popular since the 1940s, as well as a broad range of services including manicuring, facials, and the use of chemicals in hair.

The problem for Cornrows & Co. is that it offers none of these services. Its braiders do not provide facials or manicures, and they never use chemicals in the hair. All they do is braid hair, and they do it better than anyone else. Even if the braiders at Cornrows & Co. could obtain licenses, the business still could not operate unless the shop, its training program, and its managers all obtained separate licenses, which would force it to change the very nature of its training and operations.

Instead, Cornrows & Co. provides its employees with extensive training in the art of hairbraiding, which traces its origins back thousands of years to Africa. Training also includes extensive instruction in health, safety, and ethics. One of the ironies of the District of Columbia cosmetology law is that it requires no training or proficiency whatsoever in hairbraiding; yet it confers an exclusive monopoly upon licensed cosmetologists to lawfully offer hairbraiding as well as all other hairstyles. Another perverse consequence of the law is to drive hairbraiders underground into home-based businesses that escape the government's attention. Only little Cornrows & Co., trying to operate in the light of day, attracted the wrath of the government's regulators.

Faced with constant threats from the cosmetology board, Uqdah and Ferrell tried desperately to accommodate the regulators. They went as far as to hire a lawyer to draft model regulations for hairbraiding salons. They also applied for a limited license, which has been made available to shampooers, manicurists, and other specialists. In a 1986 letter to Mayor Marion Barry, Uqdah and Ferrell wrote,

> We have corresponded with your administrative offices on numerous occasions, to no avail; we've spoken with you both publicly and privately, with obviously no results. We're a growing business with future plans [for expansion]; but our own local government, the city in which we live, do

business, own property, vote and pay taxes, has refused and continues to refuse to recognize us as a viable business in the community. . . .

[K]eep us in mind sir, the next time you're in a meeting or the next time you speak to business leaders in our community, across the nation and around the world.

Let them know that there are two young people in your city who are determined to make it, despite the odds and obstacles placed in their path by their own city government; and be sure to tell them there is hope; that you know a successful business not too far from your office that holds out the promise of independence from the shackles of the slave mentality; that we are professionals, not drug dealers, that we are successful entrepreneurs who inspire others to be like them, not burdensome baby makers; that there are two young people in your own backyard, . . . who are not on public assistance or in public housing; that we're making our mark; and that hopefully, with your help, we didn't do it alone.

The city government responded to these pleas with continued intransigence, and finally in 1989, after nine years of harassment, it slapped the shop with a $1,000 fine. When their appeal of the fine within the District of Columbia administrative process was rejected two years later, Uqdah and Ferrell, represented by the Institute for Justice, filed a lawsuit seeking to enjoin the District's enforcement actions. The government retaliated by issuing an order to shut down the business, threatening Uqdah with criminal prosecution if he failed to do so. A last-minute temporary order by federal district court judge Stanley Sporkin, who compared the District's actions to those of the Soviet Union, prevented the government from sending Uqdah to jail.

But a few weeks later, Sporkin dismissed the lawsuit. The court conceded that Cornrows & Co. "is a well run business" that "provides a needed service to the community in an effective manner," and remarked that "in the present state of the nation's and this community's economic problems, it is difficult to understand why the District of Columbia wants to put a legitimate business out of operation."[2] But the court concluded that applicable legal precedent

[2]*Uqdah* v. *District of Columbia*, no. 91-2824, slip op. (D.D.C. February 21, 1992).

"does not permit the Court to scrutinize social or economic legislation with a fine-toothed comb," and hence the regulatory scheme was upheld without even allowing Uqdah and Ferrell a chance to prove their case at trial.[3] The beleaguered entrepreneurs promptly filed an appeal, but their livelihoods and the fate of their enterprise remained in daily jeopardy.

The plight of Taalib-Din Uqdah and Pamela Ferrell is far from unique. Similar cosmetology licensing laws exist in all 50 states, originally triggered by the depression of the 1930s and the desire of the cosmetology industry to limit competition. The laws are enforced by boards of cosmetology consisting of members of the regulated industry, whose own economic interest lies in making access to the profession as restrictive as possible. A 1985 study by the District of Columbia Bar found that the city's cosmetology profession is

> strongly overregulated, proportional to the benefits of regulation. Beauticians and beauty schools are subjected to heavy training and examination requirements that are unrelated to consumer safety and health. . . . Under the circumstances, heavy licensing and regulations for cosmetology have imposed an improper barrier to the practice of cosmetology, without offering significant consumer protection.[4]

The cosmetology regulations are illustrative of myriad oppressive licensing laws around the nation. Nearly 500 occupations, covering about 10 percent of all jobs in the country, are licensed by the states, and another 500 are regulated. Occupations subject to licensing requirements include not only the medical, legal, and other highly skilled professions but also professions in which the justification for regulation or restrictions on entry is virtually nonexistent, such as beekeeper, lightning rod salesman, shorthand reporter, fence installer, and septic tank cleaner. These laws are superimposed upon existing laws that protect consumers against fraud, unsafe or defective products, and other abuses. And many of them go far

---

[3] Ibid.

[4] *Regulation of Cosmetologists in the District of Columbia* (and accompanying summary) (Washington: District of Columbia Bar, 1985).

beyond health and safety objectives, and impose rigid and unreasonable barriers to entry into occupations and businesses.[5]

Licensing laws limit entrepreneurial opportunities and consumer choices every day in innumerable ways. Teacher certification requirements prevent highly qualified individuals from sharing their knowledge and skills with youngsters in public schools. Heavy regulations on nurse-midwives create obstacles for women who would like to have their babies at home.

The lawyer cartel is perhaps the most brazen at using the tools it knows so well to safeguard its privileged turf. If paralegals or other nonlawyer specialists give routine guidance on certain simple legal matters—ranging from bankruptcy to uncontested divorces to real estate transactions to filling out immigration forms—they are subject to prosecution for the unauthorized practice of law. As a consequence, prices for legal services remain high, while career opportunities are restricted for nonlawyers even if they demonstrably can provide the services better than lawyers.

Occupational licensing laws are only one part of the complex and pervasive regulatory maze at the state and local level of government that severely restricts economic liberty—the right of individuals to pursue legitimate businesses or professions free from excessive government interference. Many of these laws place the coercive power of government in the hands of the regulated industry, which wields it not to protect the public but to keep newcomers out.

Such laws have a devastating impact on people outside the economic mainstream, particularly minorities and the poor. It is because they establish oppressive conditions on entry into businesses and occupations that economist Walter Williams argued that these laws "discriminate against certain people," particularly "outsiders, latecomers and [the] resourceless," among whom members of minority groups "are disproportionately represented."[6] In sum, these laws are steadily cutting off the bottom rungs of the

---

[5]See S. David Young, *The Rule of Experts: Occupational Licensing in America* (Washington: Cato Institute, 1987); Simon Rottenberg, ed., *Occupational Licensure and Regulation* (Washington: American Enterprise Institute, 1980); and Benjamin Shimberg, et al., *Occupational Licensing: Practices and Policies* (Washington: Public Affairs Press, 1973).

[6]Walter Williams, *The State Against Blacks* (New York, McGraw-Hill, 1982), p. xvi.

economic ladder that traditionally have made our nation a beacon of opportunity.

Another common economic barrier is government-created monopolies for services ranging from cable television to garbage collection. Many of the monopolies involve businesses that require little capital and could provide opportunities for low-income entrepreneurs if they weren't forbidden by government.

A major example is taxicabs. In Washington, D.C., which allows relatively easy entry into the taxicab business, most of the drivers own their own companies, and most of the owners are members of minority groups. In most other cities, the taxicab business is restricted to one or a handful of companies. New York City, for instance, has not issued new taxicab medallions since before World War II. As a result, the cost of the limited licenses has risen to $100,000 or more,[7] thus making the taxicab business completely off limits to aspiring entrepreneurs with little capital.

Alfredo Santos learned the hard way that local government can make life very difficult for entrepreneurs who want to compete with holders of government franchises. Santos, a Houston taxicab driver, discovered on a trip to Mexico City a low-cost, highly efficient form of public transportation called "peseros." The peseros are small, privately owned vehicles—usually vans—that operate along fixed routes and charge a flat fee like buses but that offer the personalized service of taxicabs.

Santos imported the idea to Houston, using his cab during off-duty hours. Santos' "jitney service," as it's called in the United States, offered rides for a flat fee of one dollar along a five-mile route through a predominantly Hispanic and low-income section of the city. The service was such a popular alternative to the highly subsidized and inconvenient city bus service that before long other cab drivers started jitney businesses on the side.

But in some cities, building a better mousetrap is more likely to make one an outlaw than a millionaire. And so it was with Santos, who quickly was informed by city officials that his business was illegal under the Houston Anti-Jitney Law of 1924. Back toward the beginning of the century, Model-T jitneys provided aggressive

---

[7]Deidre Carmody, "Taxi Medallion Cost Pushed to $100,000 By Heavy Demand," *New York Times,* December 16, 1985.

competition for subsidized electric streetcars. (They also provided a means for black-owned companies to circumvent "separate but equal" streetcar laws.) Rather than try to win the competition in the marketplace, the streetcar companies used their leverage in city hall. By the mid-1920s, jitneys were outlawed in virtually every city except Atlantic City, where they continue to flourish today.

Seventy years later, the streetcars are long gone but the laws excluding jitneys remain. Jitneys are a mainstay of privately owned public transportation in congested cities throughout Asia and Latin America. But jitney services and the low-capital entrepreneurial opportunities they represent are illegal in this country, with the anti-jitney laws now perpetuated by the public transportation monopolies that took the place of the streetcars.[8] Meanwhile, Alfredo Santos, forced to shelve his entrepreneurial aspirations for the duration, awaits the result of a legal challenge to Houston's anti-jitney law.

Although they do so today with impunity, local governments never were intended to have power to prohibit legitimate enterprises or to arbitrarily limit entry into professions. To the contrary, economic liberty was foremost among the privileges or immunities encompassed within the protection of the Fourteenth Amendment when it was adopted in 1868. The post–Civil War black codes enacted by southern governments were designed to prevent newly emancipated blacks from competing with whites in trades and professions. The Reconstruction Congress responded by passing the Civil Rights Act of 1866, establishing federal protection for such basic civil rights as freedom of contract and private-property ownership. Concerns over the law's constitutionality impelled Congress to incorporate these protections within a constitutional amendment.

But only four years later, in the *Slaughter-House Cases*,[9] the Supreme Court ruled by a 5-4 vote that economic liberty was not encompassed within the privileges or immunities of citizenship protected against state interference by the Fourteenth Amendment. This ruling spurred oppressive state and local governments to enact

---

[8]See John M. Emshwiller, "Agencies Block Competition by Small Firms," *Wall Street Journal*, July 26, 1989, p. B1.

[9]83 U.S. 36 (1872).

onerous restrictions on entry into trades and businesses, of which occupational licensing laws and government-conferred monopolies are modern-day examples.[10]

For a brief period from the late 19th century until the 1930s, the Supreme Court struck down a number of economic regulations under the Fourteenth Amendment's due process and equal protection clauses. But this judicial protection of economic liberty came to an abrupt end with the New Deal. Since that time, according to Leonard Levy, the "Court has abdicated the responsibility of judicial review," literally singling out economic liberty for nonprotection.[11] The Court's precedents, Levy explains, establish that "if an economic right is involved, the Court never questions the reasonableness of the government's means [of achieving its objectives]. Economic rights, especially those of individuals, are inferior rights."[12]

The 1976 Supreme Court decision in *New Orleans* v. *Dukes* is a good example. The case involved a city ordinance that banned all hotdog pushcarts in the French Quarter except those that had been operated by their owners for at least eight years. Under the law, two pushcarts were allowed to remain, but Nancy Dukes' business, which had provided her livelihood for two years, alone was forced to shut down. Upholding the ordinance, the unanimous Supreme Court decision declared that "when local economic regulation is challenged solely as violating the Equal Protection Clause, this Court consistently defers to legislative determinations as to the desirability of particular statutory discriminations."[13] As Levy observed,

> If Nancy Dukes had been a nude dancer in one of the strip joints in the French Quarter and the City Council had put her out of business, she might have pleaded freedom of expression under the first amendment. Nude dancing can

---

[10]See Clint Bolick, *Unfinished Business: A Civil Rights Strategy for America's Third Century* (San Francisco: Pacific Research Institute, 1990), pp. 47–91.

[11]Leonard W. Levy, "Property as a Human Right," *Constitutional Commentary* 5 (1988): 169, 170.

[12]Ibid.

[13]*New Orleans* v. *Dukes*, 427 U.S. 297, 303 (1976).

be symbolic free speech, but selling hot dogs is just commerce, and therefore subject to little constitutional respect,
even if it involves one's livelihood.[14]

Excessive government economic regulations do not merely burden entrepreneurs who are launching or operating enterprises.
Now they're also aimed at preventing businesses from moving or
shutting down. The state of New Jersey, seeking to saddle businesses with the costs of its own regulatory blunders, passed a law
preventing certain insurance companies from leaving a business
that has become unprofitable. The situation arose from a 1983 state
law, the Automobile Full Insurance Availability Act, that sought
to provide insurance for high-risk drivers at the same cost as for
low-risk drivers. The low-cost insurance for high-risk drivers would
be provided by a Joint Underwriting Association (JUA), a government entity administered by private companies and subsidized
through traffic fines and surcharges on insurance policies.

The law proved to be a travesty. The subsidized rates for high-
risk drivers attracted people to the JUA, and by 1988 over half the
state's motorists were participants. The subsidies were inadequate,
and by 1990 the JUA had amassed a deficit of over $3.3 billion.

That year, the legislature passed a reform act, imposing $160
million in annual assessments on insurance companies while adding an additional 5 percent surtax on insurance policies, costs that
the companies were forbidden to pass along to consumers in the
form of premium hikes. To prevent companies from fleeing the
now-unprofitable insurance market, the state retroactively made it
unlawful to surrender a license to sell insurance without permission
from the commissioner of insurance, who could attach "conditions"
to such a withdrawal.

One company, Twin City Fire Insurance Company, calculated it
would lose $46.3 million in three years if the law passed, and
surrendered its license in anticipation of the legislation. After the
reform act passed, the state obtained an injunction forcing the
company to stay in business. The commissioner of insurance then
imposed 14 conditions on Twin City if it were to withdraw from
the automobile insurance industry business in the state. Among
other requirements, the company would have to continue selling

[14]Levy, p. 169.

automobile insurance for five years and even take on new clients, despite projected losses of $100 million as a result of doing so; it would have to cease selling all other types of insurance when it withdrew from the automobile market; and five other insurance companies owned by Twin City's parent corporation, ITT Hartford, would also have to withdraw from all insurance business in the state at the same time.

Twin City challenged the state's actions in court, only to have the New Jersey Supreme Court uphold the reform act and the conditions imposed on Twin City by the commissioner of insurance. The U.S. Supreme Court in 1993 refused to review the New Jersey court's decision. As a consequence, businesses and consumers in New Jersey will continue to bear tremendous costs and endure a regulatory nightmare of the state's creation.

The New Jersey example has broader ramifications as well. Even the strongest proponents of states' rights usually concede that people must be free to exit from governments they deem oppressive. The New Jersey law nullifies that basic right. "If there is no right of exit—no right to withdraw one's services in response to oppressive state legislation—then the practical ability of states to oppress their people will be vastly advanced," University of Chicago law professor Michael McConnell argues. "Berlin Walls are built for a purpose."[15]

Fortunately, judicial protection for economic liberty has experienced a bit of a renaissance in recent years. Federal courts, particularly below the Supreme Court level, have begun to question the dichotomy between judicial review of economic rights and of non-economic rights, and to subject local economic regulations to greater (though still modest) scrutiny. In 1980, the Fifth Circuit Court of Appeals struck down a Mesquite, Texas, ordinance that banned minors from coin-operated amusement arcades. The city had encouraged an arcade to open in Mesquite. But after the business opened and its owners had made a substantial financial investment, the city passed the law, which wiped out a major portion of the arcade's business.

---

[15]See Brief Amicus Curiae for the Institute for Justice, et al., in Support of the Petition for Writ of Certiorari in *Twin City Fire Insurance Co., et al., v. Fortunato*, at 7 (U.S.) No. 92-728. Professor McConnell was the primary author of the institute's brief.

The court concluded the ordinance was not rationally related to a legitimate government objective. Rather, the court found that the law was motivated by the city's disapproval of amusement arcades. "Such disapproval may justify private action, such as the withholding of patronage," the court declared, "but mere disapproval is not enough constitutionally to justify bringing the full weight of the municipality's regulatory apparatus into play."[16]

The court added,

> Our dissatisfaction with this situation, however, extends far beyond the specific incidents of this case to the entire approach to governmental regulation of personal liberty of which Mesquite's ordinance is but a sample. We certainly have no wish to challenge the legitimacy of many, even most of the statutes, ordinances and regulations issued by the innumerable legislatures and agencies in our modern and complex society. . . . Nevertheless, recognition of the multiple problems and needs of our contemporary world does not oblige us to discard the basic principles of constitutional government. . . . Executives and legislatures, from the nation's capital to the smallest village, and most of all the people themselves, are called upon by our Constitution to respect, enforce and cherish these principles of liberty and personal autonomy.[17]

Revolutions often start from the ground up, and the revolution to restore economic liberty may have started literally at that level with Ego Brown's shoeshine stands. In the mid-1980s, Brown was toiling as a bureaucrat for the U.S. Navy, all the while aspiring to start his own business. Drawing upon entrepreneurial memories from his childhood, Brown created the "Ego Shine" business, opening a shoeshine stand on a streetcorner of Washington, D.C. Before long, business was booming. Brown decided to expand and to recruit shoeshine artists from the ranks of the homeless, for whom he provided training, showers, shoeshine equipment—and a chance to lift themselves up by their bootstraps and recover their dignity.

[16]*Aladdin's Castle, Inc.* v. *City of Mesquite*, 630 F.2d 1029, 1040-46 (5th Cir. 1980), *rev'd in part and remanded*, 455 U.S. 283 (1982), *opinion extended*, 713 F.2d 137 (5th Cir. 1983).

[17]Ibid.

But the District of Columbia government found this activity intolerable and shut down Ego Brown's stands, citing a 1905 Jim Crow–era law that forbade shoeshines on the public streets. Brown's pleas to his elected representatives to lift the barrier went unheeded. Unable to support his family by shining shoes indoors, Brown teetered at the edge of the welfare rolls.

But he also went to court, and ended up striking a major blow for economic liberty. "A court would be shirking its most basic duty," declared federal district court judge John H. Pratt, "if it abstained from both an analysis of the legislation's articulated objective and the method that the legislature employed to achieve that objective."[18] Concluding that "we would have to 'strain our imagination' . . . to justify prohibiting bootblacks from the use of public space while permitting access to virtually every other type of vendor," the court struck down the law as unconstitutional.[19]

Under this precedent, many government-imposed economic barriers, particularly those that impose especially harsh burdens on some people but not on others, could be struck down. The ruling in *Brown* v. *Barry* gives hope to aspiring entrepreneurs who want to claim the basic economic liberty that is every American's birthright. Ego Brown became a symbol of the great tradition of bootstraps capitalism, and for his crusade against city hall, he was chosen ABC-TV's "Person of the Week." And as a result of Ego Brown's small triumph, as "World News Tonight" anchorman Peter Jennings declared, "He's made us all a little bit freer."

Still, the quest to restore judicial protection for economic liberty has a long way to go. Perhaps the spectacle of courageous eastern European people freeing themselves from the yoke of communism will inspire our own nation to make good on its promise of economic opportunity. To do so will require us to confront a particularly pernicious form of grassroots tyranny, but the cause could not be more vital. For it means vindicating what Justice Stephen Field once called "one of the most sacred and imprescriptible rights of man"[20]—the right to earn a living.

[18]*Brown* v. *Barry*, 710 F. Supp. 352, 355-56 (D.D.C. 1989).
[19]Ibid.
[20]*Slaughter-House Cases*, 83 U.S. 36, 110 (Field, J., dissenting).

9. Privacy

Most Americans believe that their home is their castle. The sanctity of the home is a cherished tradition. We can keep unwelcome intruders out by resorting to the trespass laws. Government is not exempt from these limitations; several provisions of the Constitution explicitly protect people and their property against unwarranted government intrusions. What happens inside the home generally is no one's business but that of the people who live there.

At least that's what Michael Hardwick thought, until he discovered harsh reality. On August 3, 1982, Hardwick was arrested for having sex with another man in the bedroom of his own home. Hardwick was prosecuted under Georgia's anti-sodomy law, which provides that a "person commits the offense of sodomy when he performs or submits to any sexual act involving the sex organs of one person and the mouth or anus of another." The law further provides that a "person convicted of the offense of sodomy shall be punished by imprisonment for not less than one nor more than 20 years."[1]

Hardwick's nightmarish ordeal took him, four years later, all the way to the U.S. Supreme Court. There he invoked well-established constitutional principles that recognize a zone of privacy around individuals and their property.[2] But Hardwick was in for a shock: by a 5-4 vote, the Court upheld the law. Hardwick faced losing up to two decades of his life for a consensual act that harmed no one and took place in the privacy of his own bedroom.

Gays are not the only people with something to fear from the Georgia morals police. The broad sweep of the state's anti-sodomy law proscribes not only homosexual acts but also acts commonly engaged in by heterosexual couples. Unfortunately for Hardwick, his homosexuality permitted Justice Byron White, writing for the majority, to cast the issue as "whether the Federal Constitution

[1]Ga. Code Ann. sec. 16-6-2.
[2]*Bowers* v. *Hardwick*, 478 U.S. 186, 190–96 (1986).

153

confers a fundamental right" upon "homosexuals to engage in acts of sodomy." The majority found that the Constitution protects only those rights " 'implicit in the concept of ordered liberty' " or that are " 'deeply rooted in this Nation's history and tradition.' " Previously recognized rights protected within the realm of privacy, the Court noted, included child rearing and education, family relationships, procreation, marriage, contraception, and abortion. But none of these rights, White declared, "bears any resemblance to the claimed constitutional right of homosexuals" to have sex. Because no fundamental right was involved, the Court concluded the government need only demonstrate a "rational basis" for the law. To this end, the Court found adequate the "majority sentiments about the morality of homosexuality" reflected by the law."

The four dissenters vehemently disagreed. Michael Hardwick was not asserting a fundamental right to engage in homosexual sodomy, Justice Harry Blackmun observed. In reality, Blackmun declared, "this case is about 'the most comprehensive of rights and the right most valued by civilized man,' namely, 'the right to be let alone.' "[3]

Quoting Louis Brandeis, Blackmun recounted, " 'Our cases have long recognized that the Constitution embodies a promise that a certain sphere of individual liberty will be kept largely beyond the reach of government.' " This concept of privacy, Blackmun explained, is based on the " 'moral fact that a person belongs to himself and not to others nor to society as a whole.' " If this constitutional guarantee "means anything," Blackmun reasoned, "it means that, before Georgia can prosecute its citizens for making choices about the most intimate aspects of their lives, it must do more than assert that the choice they have made is 'an abominable crime not fit to be named among Christians.' "[4] Nonetheless, five members of the Court found this justification sufficient to uphold the law and Hardwick's conviction.[5]

[3]Ibid., p. 199 (Blackmun, J., dissenting) (citing *Olmstead* v. *United States*, 277 U.S. 438, 478 (1928) (Brandeis, J., dissenting).

[4]Ibid. at 199–203.

[5]The deciding vote was cast by Justice Lewis Powell, who remarked after he retired that he regretted his vote in this case, which surely provides small comfort to Michael Hardwick.

The Georgia law under which Hardwick was charged is no aberration: sodomy, defined to encompass both oral and anal sex, is illegal in 24 states and the District of Columbia. Some states prohibit other common consensual relationships and sex acts. Virginia, for example, proscribes all voluntary sexual intercourse between unmarried persons as well as "lewd and lascivious" cohabitation of unmarried persons.[6] The penalties can be severe. Rhode Island's anti-sodomy law provides for between 7 and 20 years imprisonment; Montana's statute provides for a 10-year prison term and/or a $50,000 fine.

Enforcement of the laws often produces perverse effects. They are sometimes used as weapons for the unscrupulous to exact revenge for relationships that have gone sour. During a bitter divorce trial, a Georgia woman charged her husband, James Moseley, with rape. The jury found that the act was consensual and therefore acquitted Moseley of rape. But because Moseley admitted he had performed oral sex with his wife, he was convicted of sodomy and sentenced to two years in prison. Similar cases have arisen under anti-sodomy laws in other states.[7]

The word "privacy" does not appear in the Constitution, giving fuel to arguments that the Framers did not intend to give privacy rights constitutional protection. This view holds that the Constitution protects only those rights explicitly enumerated. Even if that restrictive view of individual liberty were correct, however, one could easily find protection for privacy in the Constitution. For privacy rights as we now understand them are an inherent component of property rights, which are explicitly protected by the Constitution.[8] The Third, Fourth, Fifth, and Fourteenth Amendments safeguard people and property against government intrusions in a variety of ways: they restrict government from military occupation of homes, they protect people and their property against unreasonable searches and seizures, they prohibit the taking of property for

[6]Va. Code sec. 18.2-344-345.

[7]Charles Oliver, "Georgia on My Mind," *Reason* (October 1989), p. 14. See also Lisa Leff, "Md. Court Hears Appeal of Oral Sex Conviction," *Washington Post*, April 28, 1990, p. B1.

[8]For an insightful treatment of the historical and philosophical connection between property and privacy rights, see Mary Chlopecki, "The Property Rights Origins of Privacy Rights," *The Freeman* (August 1992), pp. 306-9.

public use except with just compensation, and they limit government's power to intrude upon property without due process of law. Moreover, the protection of individual liberty in the First, Ninth, and Fourteenth Amendments encompasses a realm of individual autonomy that government may not properly invade.

The Court's decision in *Bowers* v. *Hardwick* marked a significant departure from a long line of precedents protecting privacy of the home and family. In *Pierce* v. *Society of Sisters*[9] in 1925, for instance, the Supreme Court invalidated an Oregon law requiring parents to send their children to public schools only, holding that parents have the right to direct the education of their children. In its decision 40 years later in *Griswold* v. *Connecticut*,[10] the Court struck down a statute forbidding the sale and use of contraceptives as a violation of the privacy right attending the marital relationship.

Consistent with the overriding constitutional value of privacy, the Court has protected activities taking place in the privacy of the home that permissibly are criminalized if they take place elsewhere. Four years after *Griswold*, the Court extended the privacy protection to another "victimless crime" in *Stanley* v. *Georgia*. In that case, police raided the home of Robert Stanley seeking evidence of illegal gambling activities. They uncovered no such evidence, but found in Stanley's bedroom drawers three reels of film. Using a projector they took from Stanley's living room, the police played the films and decided they were obscene. Stanley was convicted under state law for the felony of "knowingly having possession of . . . obscene material."

The Supreme Court overturned the conviction. The government may permissibly prohibit the sale or manufacture of obscene materials, the Court acknowledged. But as Justice Thurgood Marshall declared in his majority opinion, "A State has no business telling a man, sitting alone in his own house, what books he may read or what films he may watch. Our whole constitutional heritage rebels at the thought of giving government the power to control men's minds."[11]

---

[9]268 U.S. 510 (1925).
[10]381 U.S. 479 (1965).
[11]*Stanley* v. *Georgia*, 394 U.S. 557, 565 (1969).

The markedly different philosophies embodied in cases such as *Pierce, Griswold,* and *Stanley* on one hand, and in the Court's sanctioning of the state's invasion of the bedroom in *Bowers* on the other, reflect a broader debate over the proper relationship between government and the individual. As Justice John Paul Stevens remarked in his *Bowers* dissent, these issues go " 'to the origins of the American heritage of freedom—the abiding interest in individual liberty that makes certain state intrusions on the citizen's right to decide how he will live his own life intolerable.' "[12]

But states' rights theorists see it differently. For many conservatives, privacy rights were created out of thin air. Robert Bork, for instance, believes that "the major freedom . . . of our kind of society is the freedom to choose to have a public morality."[13] Bork thus rejected the view that Michael Hardwick's sex acts with a male lover were a "victimless crime," in that "knowledge that an activity is taking place is a harm to those who find it profoundly immoral." Bork granted "that statement will be taken as repressive by many, but only because they really do not disapprove of the conduct."[14]

In Robert Bork's philosophy, the fact that conduct is consensual and takes place in one's own home is irrelevant. As long as the invasion of privacy necessary to stamp out the offensive conduct is clothed with the imprimatur of majority approval, the courts are powerless to stop it. And those who object to criminalizing such conduct or to the civil liberties consequences attending the enforcement of such laws cannot be sincere in their beliefs; their true motivation is that they approve of the conduct.

Ironically, one of the best responses to Robert Bork's current majoritarian thinking was provided by Bork himself in a 1963 article on proposed civil rights legislation. Whenever "the morals of the majority are self-righteously imposed upon a minority," Bork argued, the "discussion we ought to hear is of the cost in freedom that must be paid for such legislation, the morality of enforcing

---

[12]*Bowers,* at 217 (Stevens, J., dissenting).

[13]Robert H. Bork, *Tradition and Morality in Constitutional Law* (Washington: American Enterprise Institute for Public Policy Research, 1984), p. 9.

[14]Robert H. Bork, *The Tempting of America* (New York: Free Press, 1990), p. 185.

morals through law, and the likely consequences for law enforcement of trying to do so."[15] Bork declared,

> The principle of such legislation is that if I find your behavior ugly by my standards, moral or aesthetic, and if you prove stubborn about adopting my view of the situation, I am justified in having the state coerce you into more righteous paths. That is itself a principle of unsurpassed ugliness.[16]

Unfortunately, the Supreme Court's *Bowers* decision lends precedential credence to this "principle of unsurpassed ugliness," thereby giving local governments virtual carte blanche in matters of social regulation.

Nowhere is the zeal to stamp out individual autonomy in the name of public morality more pronounced than in the so-called war on drugs being waged by every level of government. As in most wars, precious civil liberties are too frequently lost in the fray. Individuals are arrested for victimless offenses, invasions of private places are sanctioned, assets of innocent people are seized, many of those convicted are sentenced to mandatory minimum prison terms far out of proportion to the offenses they've committed, the profits of organized crime are inflated, and scarce police resources are diverted away from crimes against people and property.

The massive deployment of police resources and willingness to violate civil liberties often does not depend upon the severity of the offense. The casual, harmless drug user is at as great a risk as the murderous drug lord. Indeed, the practice of seizing private property has made drug raids profitable to law enforcement officials, a phenomenon that has raised the ire even of the conservative *Washington Times*. A 1991 police raid of a University of Virginia fraternity house that netted a few hundred dollars worth of drugs— a bust the *Washington Times* characterized as "the law enforcement equivalent of a panty raid"—nonetheless resulted in the seizure by police of three entire houses worth $1 million that weren't even owned by the students. As the newspaper editorialized,

> Busting frat rats and other small time pushers is not exactly a strategic move in the war on drugs, but it does seem to

[15]Robert H. Bork, "Civil Rights—A Challenge," *The New Republic*, August 31, 1963, pp. 21–22.
[16]Ibid.

pay well for the cops who carry it out. Meanwhile, murder and rape rates are soaring. Padding the budgets of underfed police departments with the private property of innocent people does nothing to punish the guilty or stop them from poisoning America with illicit drugs.[17]

One of the most sweeping, and least justified, drug raids took place in 1990 in Tazewell County, Illinois. One Friday morning, well-coordinated teams of state police, sheriff's deputies, local police, and drug-sniffing dogs simultaneously converged upon eight local high schools. Ten thousand lockers and automobiles in surrounding neighborhoods were sniffed and some were searched, while all the students were detained in the schools for as long as two hours. There were no prior indications of drug dealing or possession in the high schools, and indeed few if any drugs were found. Rather, the police wanted to see if they could pull off the raid and "to find out if there was a problem," explained Sheriff James Donahue. "You never know until you go in to take a look."[18]

But courts are increasingly reluctant to interpose themselves between overzealous police and individual citizens. The *Washington Post* reported in 1990 that a survey of 200 cases revealed that "judges are routinely upholding the legality of [drug] searches," even of people who fit no "profile" but are "stopped simply at random in bus, train, or air terminals."[19] If government is allowed to pursue its war on drugs regardless of the cost to civil liberties, we may one day find that the price paid for this war is the loss of our privacy.

Not all privacy cases, however, deal with illegal drugs, homosexuality, pornography, or other behavior legislatively deemed socially deviant. Sometimes they involve merely an ordinary family trying peacefully to live together.

In early 1973, Mrs. Inez Moore, an elderly black woman, was prosecuted on criminal charges and sentenced to five days in jail and a $25 fine. Her crime was having an "illegal occupant" in her

[17]"Property of the State," *Washington Times*, April 4, 1991, p. G2.

[18]Nat Hentoff, "The Day All the County's Kids Were in Custody," *Washington Post*, August 18, 1990, p. A21.

[19]Tracy Thompson, "4th Amendment Is Trampled in Drug Offensive, Critics Say," *Washington Post*, May 7, 1990, p. A1.

East Cleveland home: her grandson, John, who came to live with Mrs. Moore when his mother died. By having two grandchildren living in her home who were cousins rather than brothers, Mrs. Moore violated a local ordinance limiting residences to "family" occupancy. "Family" was defined extremely narrowly to encompass only traditional "nuclear" families; that is, the owners, their parents, and their children. Indeed, under the East Cleveland law, not even adult siblings could lawfully reside together.[20]

The city justified the ordinance on the grounds of traffic congestion and undue financial burden on the schools. But Justice Lewis Powell, writing for a plurality of the Court, found that "while these are legitimate goals, the ordinance before us serves them marginally, at best."[21] The law was both overbroad and underinclusive in that it prohibited families (like unmarried adult siblings) who would not cause traffic congestion or burden the schools, while allowing families with several children who would contribute to such problems. Moreover, Powell stated, the Court's precedents "have consistently acknowledged a 'private realm of family life which the state cannot enter,' " requiring the Court to "examine carefully" the government's purposes and methods whenever it "intrudes on choices concerning family living arrangements." Under such scrutiny, Powell concluded, "this ordinance cannot survive."[22]

For Justice Stevens, the issue presented in the case was more straightforward: the "critical question," Stevens declared in his opinion concurring with the majority, "is whether East Cleveland's housing ordinance is a permissible restriction on [Mrs. Moore's] right to use her own property as she sees fit."[23] He concluded there was no justification for the city's ordinance, with the result that the law "constitutes a taking of property without due process and without just compensation."

---

[20]In response to a question from Sen. Joseph Biden about the *Moore* case, Justice Clarence Thomas noted at his confirmation hearing that when he was a youngster in rural Georgia, his family could not have met the standards of the East Cleveland ordinance.

[21]*Moore* v. *City of East Cleveland*, 431 U.S. 494, 499-500 (1977) (plurality).

[22]Ibid.

[23]Ibid., at 513, 520–21 (Stevens, J., concurring in the judgment).

The *Moore* decision would seem an easy one, whether decided on privacy grounds or on the property rights from which privacy rights are derived. But Mrs. Moore escaped a jail term only by the slimmest of margins, with four justices dissenting, and with a majority unable to agree on a basis for striking down the ordinance. Further confusing the state of privacy rights, the Court only three years earlier had upheld a zoning law that forbade unrelated persons from living together[24]—an ordinance that could hardly have a more rational justification than the one struck down in *Moore*. The right to privacy rests on a slender reed if it depends on such constitutional hair-splitting.

More ominously, the changing composition of the Supreme Court since the *Moore* decision may mean greater support for the Bork view that any social regulation is permissible if it reflects majoritarian moral sentiment. Can it be that our privacy and property rights have been eroded to such an extent that a city today could indeed make a grandmother go to jail for providing a home for her grandson?

Those who would sanction such acts have their constitutional law confused. When government invades the personal life of an individual, the burden should not be placed on the individual to justify his or her actions; the burden should be on the government to justify its actions. That does not mean the government can never regulate social behavior. Indeed, the less private the behavior and the greater its impact on third parties, the greater the justification for reasonable government regulation.

But if government's power to control people's lives is not bounded even by the sanctity of a person's home and the consensual, nonharmful acts that go on inside it, then government's power is not really bounded at all. Our nation's legacy of freedom will depend in large measure on whether the Supreme Court continues to recognize that there are some aspects of individuals' lives into which government has no business intruding—and acts to preserve the precious privacy that is a cornerstone of our free society.

[24]*Village of Belle Terre* v. *Boraas*, 416 U.S. 1 (1974).

10. Equality under Law

In May 1987, Mrs. Mary Amaya received a certified letter from John P. Andreassen, psychologist for the Fontana, California, Unified Schools, containing distressing news. It read in part:

> Dear Mrs. Amaya:
>
> Your son, Demond Crawford, has been recommended for testing in intellectual, academic, and other areas as a possible candidate for special placement because of poor performance in academic areas.
>
> I am enclosing an Assessment Plan with areas designating tests to be given. . . .
>
> Once I have completed testing, I will ask you to come to Alder Junior High to discuss the test results and to decide on the most appropriate placement for your child.[1]

But even more disturbing than the body of the letter was the brief postscript: "Because Demond is Black, we will be unable to give him an intelligence test."

Mrs. Amaya was incredulous. What did her son's race have to do with his opportunity to take a test that could help determine the nature or extent of his academic difficulties? Mrs. Amaya contacted the school district to complain, but learned that the postscript was no fluke. It was official state policy, she was informed, to prohibit black youngsters from taking standardized intelligence tests. But there was a simple solution, according to the school officials: because Demond Crawford was half Hispanic, Mrs. Amaya could merely "reregister" Demond as Hispanic instead of black, and the school district would administer the test.

Mrs. Amaya refused to compromise her son's ethnicity merely to satisfy some social engineering bureaucrat. "I have raised my son to believe that the color of his skin didn't make any difference

[1] *Larry P.* v. *Riles*, 495 F. Supp. 926 (N.D. Cal. 1979).

163

as to what he could do or accomplish," she declared, adding that Demond "has grown up and competed in school and sports with Black kids, Hispanic kids and white kids." But now, "for the first time in his life, he has been told he can't do something—take an intelligence test—because he is Black. And it is the State of California that is telling him he can't. I don't agree!"

The state policy denying Demond access to testing on account of his race was an outgrowth of a 1979 federal court order barring the state from using standardized intelligence tests to identify black children as "educable mentally retarded" (E.M.R.) or to place them in special E.M.R. classes. The state denied the tests were discriminatory, and continued after the court ruling to make them available for children of other colors and for other types of learning problems.

But seven years after the court order, under pressure from liberal special-interest groups, the state reversed course and extended the ban on standardized intelligence tests to all black schoolchildren for all special education services. A December 3, 1986, directive implementing the new policy was issued by Bill Honig, state superintendent of public instruction. Honig's directive was like something out of Orwell:

> An I.Q. test may not be given to a Black pupil even with parental consent. . . .
>
> The following reasons are *not* permissible justifications for the administration of an I.Q. test to a Black pupil:
>
> 1) As part of a comprehensive plan to which a parent has consented;
> 2) To gain diagnostic information;
> 3) To develop goals and objectives;
> 4) To determine a special education pupil's educational needs;
> 5) To develop a pupil's strengths and weaknesses as elicited by the I.Q. test.

The state's policy took social engineering to a remarkable new extreme. Rather than merely restricting the test to valid purposes, the state imposed a blanket ban, and used race as the sole criterion. If Demond were white, Asian, American Indian, Hispanic, or any ethnicity other than African-American, he would be allowed to take the I.Q. test. But because he was black, the state blocked access to the test, regardless of the purpose for which his mother wanted to use it.

Nor were Demond's circumstances unique. Herb and Nan Condit sought an I.Q. test for their 8½-year-old son Gary, who seemed like a bright youngster but was reading at a five-year-old level. The Condits encountered the same policy as Mary Amaya: since one of Gary's parents was black, he was prohibited from taking the test. As Mrs. Condit recounts,

> The school district went on to tell me that since Gary was neither white nor black (due to his mixed parentage), that if I wanted to change the school registration card to say "white," I could. My husband and I talked it over and were torn between our principles and our desire to see Gary receive the testing he needs. In the end, our principles won out. It is infuriating to realize that there is a law like this in this day and age! If we had listed Gary as white, he could have the test—but if we listed him as black, he could not— yet he is the same child!

The Condits had Gary tested privately and found he had a high I.Q., which confirmed their suspicion that his academic problems were not intelligence-related. But because of the state's blacks-only I.Q. test ban, the school district would not even make Gary's test results a part of his record, or take them into account in mapping out a course of action to address his difficulties.[2]

Little Gary Condit certainly was not the first person the government has treated differently on account of his skin color. In perhaps the most famous such instance, nearly a hundred years before the state of California told Gary Condit and Demond Crawford they could not have access to a publicly administered test because they are half black, Adolph Plessy was imprisoned for trying to board a railroad car reserved for whites because he was one-eighth black. It was not the railroad company that wanted to consign Plessy to a segregated car, however, but rather the state government, which

---

[2]See Memorandum of Points and Authorities in Support of Plaintiffs' Motion for Preliminary Injunction and supporting exhibits in *Crawford* v. *Honig*, No. C-89-0014 RFP (N.D. Calif., motion filed April 4, 1991), and Clint Bolick, *Unfinished Business: A Civil Rights Strategy for America's Third Century* (San Francisco: Pacific Research Institute, 1990), pp. 93–95.

forced private companies to provide "separate but equal" accommodations. Indeed, the Louisiana and Nashville Railroad funded a test case to challenge the law, but Plessy's conviction was upheld by the U.S. Supreme Court, unleashing a regime of invidious government discrimination that survives to this day. Lamenting the infamous 1896 decision in *Plessy* v. *Ferguson*, Justice John Harlan, the sole dissenter, wrote,

> Our Constitution is color-blind, and neither knows nor tolerates classes among citizens. In respect of civil rights, all citizens are equal before the law. The humblest is the peer of the most powerful. The law regards man as man, and takes no account of his surroundings or of his color when his civil rights as guaranteed by the supreme law of the land are involved. It is therefore to be regretted that this high tribunal, the final expositor of the fundamental law of the land, has reached the conclusion that it is competent for a state to regulate the enjoyment by citizens of their civil rights solely upon the basis of race.[3]

The *Plessy* decision eviscerated the Fourteenth Amendment's guarantee to all citizens of "equal protection of the laws." Following the Civil War, southern state legislators enacted pernicious laws designed to deprive newly emancipated blacks of such basic rights as freedom of contract, property rights, and economic liberty. To better protect these rights, the equal protection clause was added to the Constitution to counteract the evil of "factions"—today known as special-interest groups—that manipulate the power of government for their own ends. Properly construed, the equal protection guarantee means that any time a state or local government classifies people or assigns different benefits or burdens to them, it must demonstrate that its discriminatory treatment has a rational basis. Because it is almost never rational for government to discriminate on the basis of race, race is the most suspect of classifications.

But unfortunately, Justice Harlan's view of the Fourteenth Amendment has never been embraced by a majority of the Supreme Court, and government all too often has persuaded the courts that invidious discrimination of one kind or another is legitimate.

[3]*Plessy* v. *Ferguson*, 163 U.S. 537, 559 (1896) (Harlan, J., dissenting).

166

Perhaps the most shameful example was the internment of citizens of Japanese ancestry during World War II, which the Supreme Court upheld on the basis of perceived emergency conditions. In his prophetic dissent, Justice Robert Jackson warned that

> a judicial construction . . . that will sustain this order is a far more subtle blow to liberty than the promulgation of the order itself. . . . [O]nce a judicial order rationalizes . . . the Constitution to show that [it] sanctions such an order, the Court for all time has validated the principle of racial discrimination. . . . The principle then lies about like a loaded weapon ready for the hand of any authority that can bring forward a plausible claim of an urgent need.[4]

Justice Jackson's prescience has been confirmed repeatedly in the half-century since he penned those words. Most people probably believe that official discrimination by government on the basis of race was curbed by *Brown* v. *Board of Education*, the 1964 Civil Rights Act, and subsequent laws and judicial decisions. But unfortunately, such official discrimination persists. And as in the past, departures from the principle of equality under law now occur most often at the state and local levels of government. As Justice Antonin Scalia has observed, "The struggle for racial justice has historically been a struggle by the national society against oppression in the individual States. . . . And the struggle retains that character in modern times."[5] As Scalia explains,

> Experience shows that racial discrimination against any group finds a more ready expression at the state and local level than at the federal level. To the children of the Founding Fathers, this should come as no surprise. An acute danger of oppression in small, rather than large, political units dates back to the very beginning of our national history.[6]

As if to prove Scalia's point, instances of racial discrimination for social engineering purposes, such as California's blacks only

---

[4]*Korematsu* v. *United States*, 323 U.S. 214 (1944).

[5]*City of Richmond* v. *J. A. Croson Co.*, 109 S.Ct. 706, 736–737 (1989) (Scalia, J., concurring in the judgment).

[6]Ibid.

I.Q. test ban, are plentiful at the state and local levels, and they often end up harming the very people they are intended to benefit. Some examples:

- Public housing authorities in Starrett City, N.Y., and elsewhere have engaged in so-called integration maintenance policies, in which public housing units are kept vacant—despite long waiting lists of black applicants—in the hope that white families will rent the apartments and thereby preserve racial balance.[7]
- State social services agencies sometimes prevent orphaned black children from being adopted by loving families of different ethnicities, leaving the children hostage to an often uncaring foster care system.[8]
- Prince George's County, Maryland, and other school districts involuntarily transfer both black and white teachers on the basis of skin color so as to preserve racial balance among the faculty of each school, even if the teachers have been in the schools for many years and are not qualified to teach the new subjects to which they're assigned.[9]

In situations like these, government officials, often acting under pressure from special-interest groups, assign a higher value to amorphous race-oriented goals than to either the principle of equality under law or to the best interests of the people they're supposed to serve.

But if new justifications have surfaced for these modern types of racial classifications, classic forms of discrimination still persist, even with massive resources deployed to enforce antidiscrimination laws at the national, state, and local levels. Despite increased public consciousness about the evils and irrationality of race discrimination, people are all too often still willing to use the coercive power of government to redistribute benefits to some and burdens to others on the basis of race.

---

[7]*United States* v. *Starrett City Associates*, 840 F.2d 1096 (2d Cir. 1988).

[8]Lynne Duke, "Couples Challenging Same-Race Adoption Policies," *Washington Post*, April 5, 1992, pp. A1, A6.

[9]*Vaughns* v. *Prince George's County Board of Education*, 742 F. Supp. 1275 (D. Md. 1990).

Such was the case until recently in Yonkers, New York, a city whose government was as repressive against blacks as many of the worst southern governments of the Jim Crow era. A large suburb adjacent to New York City, Yonkers is traversed by the Saw Mill River Parkway, a physical barrier that also separates black neighborhoods from white ones. Many white residents of Yonkers—concerned about the emigration of blacks from the nearby Bronx—were determined to keep it that way. Their weapon was the machinery of city government.

Until a series of federal court decisions in the mid-1980s, the city of Yonkers engaged in a series of actions and policies designed to maintain rigid racial segregation and to consign blacks to inferior housing and educational opportunities. From the 1930s until more than two decades after the Supreme Court's 1954 *Brown* v. *Board of Education* decision, school authorities deliberately manipulated attendance zone boundaries to maintain segregated schools, forcing youngsters to travel greater distances and cross dangerous thoroughfares so as to maintain racial separation. Decisions about where to construct or shut down schools depended not on the best interests of students but on the impact those decisions would have on integration. School officials "steered" black students to dead-end vocational courses in inferior schools while providing high-quality opportunities for students in predominantly white schools. Schools in predominantly black neighborhoods were decrepit, overcrowded, and staffed with less-experienced teachers. In short, a youngster's opportunity to enjoy a decent public education in Yonkers depended in large part upon whether the child was white or black.[10]

Meanwhile, the black community in Yonkers was also being victimized by the city's policies with respect to public housing projects. Justice William Brennan, writing in the context of a 1990 decision involving a remedy for the city's discriminatory actions, observed that "for the past four decades, Yonkers officials have

---

[10]*United States* v. *Yonkers Board of Education*, 624 F. Supp. 1276 (S.D.N.Y. 1985), aff'd, 837 F.2d 1181 (2d Cir. 1987), cert. denied, 486 U.S. 1055 (1988). The author was lead attorney in the Second Circuit Court of Appeals for the Department of Justice, which successfully prosecuted the city of Yonkers for housing and school segregation.

relentlessly preserved and exacerbated racial residential segregation throughout the city."[11] Between 1949 and 1982, the city approved three dozen sites for low-income public housing, all of them in or adjacent to black neighborhoods. The effect was devastating: southwest Yonkers was turned into a ghetto, with increased congestion, school overcrowding, and deterioration of housing values.

In the face of federal prosecution of discrimination in housing and education, the city of Yonkers fiercely defended its actions. The selection of sites for low-income housing, the city insisted, was based not on race but on the desire to limit such developments to low-income neighborhoods. But the evidence—which the trial court judge found "remarkably consistent and extreme"—instead demonstrated that the sites were selected by city officials in response to intense and constant political pressure by whites in Yonkers to confine blacks to isolated sections of the city.[12]

Yonkers was not required to erect any public housing at all. But once it decided to do so, and to accept federal funds to subsidize its construction, the city was constitutionally obligated to make decisions relating to public housing without regard to race. The city government could permissibly have chosen to construct public housing only in low-income neighborhoods. Instead, it chose sites only in or adjacent to black neighborhoods, whether or not those neighborhoods were primarily low-income. Out of 38 housing projects approved by the city, only 2 were outside predominantly black southwest Yonkers. One was a senior citizens project whose residents were almost all white. The other was built in Runyon Heights, a small, physically isolated middle-class black enclave in central Yonkers. Like white middle-class Yonkers citizens, the residents of Runyon Heights objected to low-income housing in their neighborhood, but the city government ignored their protests.

In making site selections, the city government overrode the recommendations of its own city planning experts, who were concerned that the extreme concentration of low-income housing in

[11]*Spallone* v. *United States*, 110 S.Ct. 625, 635 (1990) (Brennan, J., dissenting). Although the justices disagreed over the proper remedy, all agreed, in the words of Chief Justice Rehnquist, that "there can be no question about the liability of the city of Yonkers for racial discrimination." Ibid., at 631 (majority).

[12]See Clint Bolick, "Yonkers Revisited: Discrimination and Judicial Power," *Hofstra Property Law Journal* 3, (Fall 1989): 1–14.

southwest Yonkers would turn the area into a ghetto. The city repeatedly violated its own zoning and planning rules to approve projects if they were in black neighborhoods, or to reject projects if they were in white neighborhoods.

The city government's determination to maintain racial segregation was made especially clear in the early 1980s, when the federal government moved away from subsidized construction of public housing developments in favor of vouchers that would allow low-income residents to rent housing of their choice. Fearing that the vouchers would increase mobility of black residents, the city in 1982 distributed only 36 of the 120 housing vouchers allotted by the federal government, despite a waiting list of 800. The few vouchers the city distributed outside southwest Yonkers were to white families, and city officials refused to apply for additional vouchers despite a desperate housing shortage.

The federal government blew the whistle on the Yonkers government's racist housing and education policies in a lawsuit filed in 1980. But rather than find a way out of the situation, the city government engaged in massive resistance. Repeated Department of Justice compromise efforts were rejected; elected officials who tried to find a solution were turned out of office in favor of race-baiting opponents. Finally after a 100-day trial, federal district court Judge Leonard Sand found the city guilty of discrimination in housing and education. When the city government refused to voluntarily approve a remedy, Judge Sand ordered the city to construct 200 units of subsidized housing in nonminority neighborhoods.[13] The city's recalcitrance ultimately undermined the very community and property values it claimed to support.

The brazen actions of the Yonkers city government to perpetuate segregation would have made the southern white supremacists of yesteryear proud. In a sense, though, the Yonkers government was worse than its predecessors who were avowed racists, for it sought to hide its true motivations behind a facade of concern over property values and the city's well-being. Had the government exercised its democratic mandate in good faith, it could have protected such legitimate values while at the same time fulfilling its obligation of equal opportunity. Instead, it sacrificed the rights of black Yonkers

[13]*United States* v. *Yonkers Board of Education*, 635 F. Supp. 1577 (S.D.N.Y. 1986).

residents for the benefit of others; and in the process, it sacrificed everyone. The blame for the tragic saga of Yonkers lies with the city's elected officials, who violated their oaths to uphold and defend the constitutional principles that protect us all.

Yet, as if we have not learned the lessons of history well enough, recent years have witnessed an explosion of new forms of discrimination by government, with new justifications to accommodate them. Whether the rationale is affirmative action, reparations, distributive justice, cultural diversity, or some other euphemism, government programs that allocate benefits and burdens on the basis of race once again permeate American society. Like all forms of discrimination, racial preferences harm innocent individuals solely because of their race—and confer dubious benefits upon those who are preferred.[14]

In 1980, Stuart Marsh, a Flint, Michigan, public school guidance counselor, was looking forward to retiring in a few years after long and excellent service to the school district. But when reductions in force were necessary, Marsh was singled out for demotion solely because he was white. Ignoring seniority and the fact that Marsh received the highest possible ratings from white and black supervisors alike, Marsh was swept aside by a strict racial quota designed to maintain racial balance. Race had supplanted such factors as experience, merit, and educational quality as the basis for personnel decisions in the public schools.

Like Rosa Parks, who 25 years earlier was forced to surrender her seat on a public bus because of her skin color, Stuart Marsh was the wrong race at the wrong place at the wrong time. Marsh was the victim of one of thousands of racial preferences that pervade hiring, promotion, and layoff decisions by state and local governments.[15]

State and local governments also depart from the principle of equality under law by routinely awarding preferences in public contracts to "minority contractors," under a system that is often rife with corruption.[16] Likewise, public colleges and universities

[14]See Bolick, *Unfinished Business*, pp. 93–133.

[15]Marsh ultimately won a court battle with the school district after the U.S. Supreme Court remanded his case in light of *Wygant* v. *Jackson Board of Education*, 476 U.S. 267 (1986), which struck down a similar quota policy.

[16]*City of Richmond* v. *J. A. Croson Co.*, 109 S.Ct. 706 (1989).

often make admissions and faculty hiring decisions in accordance with "diversity" or "affirmative action" policies, which confer benefits upon individuals not because of socioeconomic disadvantages, but because of their color or ethnicity.[17]

Race based policies are now so firmly entrenched that some government entities suppress anyone who dissents from the official orthodoxy. Stanley Dea refused to go along—and suffered the consequences.[18] An Asian-American, Dea is employed by the Washington Suburban Sanitation Commission, a regional authority created by the governments of Montgomery and Prince George's counties in Maryland. Until April 1990, Dea was director of the Bureau of Planning and Design, a department of 250 employees. Dea's responsibilities included personnel selection and recommendations of outside contractors.

In the summer of 1988, the local chapter of the National Association for the Advancement of Colored People demanded that the commission hire more blacks in management positions and retain more minority contracting firms. The commission obliged. Dea was pressured by higher ranking commission officials to make contracting recommendations on the basis of race. Dea objected, warning that race-based contracting decisions would lead to reduced quality and higher costs—predictions that proved correct whenever the commission overrode his recommendations. Even when the commission's own lawyers advised in 1989 that the minority contracting quota policy was unlawful, the commission persisted in selecting contractors on the basis of race.

Dea was also pressured to hire and promote black engineers, regardless of relative qualifications. In July 1989, he needed to fill a project manager vacancy. The highest ranking candidate was a white female, who declined the position. Dea selected the next best qualified candidate, a white male. When Richard Hocevar, the commission's general manager, confronted Dea over his failure to hire a less-qualified minority candidate, Dea offered to readvertise

[17]See, for example, Vincent Sarich, "The Institutionalization of Racism at the University of California at Berkeley," *Academic Questions* (Winter 1990–91), p. 72; and Stephen R. Barnett, "Get Back," *New Republic*, February 18, 1991, p. 24 (describing faculty diversity policies at Berkeley).
[18]The author represents Dea in a legal challenge along with attorney Douglas Herbert. The following account is based on notes and transcripts.

the position to create a larger applicant pool, but refused to discriminate on the basis of race. Hocevar suspended Dea for five days for "gross insubordination," on the grounds that Dea was "negligent and insensitive in not selecting a minority" and "did not appreciate how important affirmative action was" to the commission.

Dea appealed his suspension, and the commission downgraded the violation to insubordination. The commission issued a written warning, which would be transferred from the active to the confidential section of Dea's file if he rendered 12 months of "problem-free service."

But in early 1990, another vacancy occurred in Dea's department. When commission officials learned that Dea's three top candidates were white males, he was involuntarily transferred to a new position in the agency—a dead-end job with no managerial or personnel responsibilities. Dea learned that in the 1990s, it is no longer politically correct, or even tolerable, to stand up for equal opportunity in certain local government agencies.

Whether visited upon whites or blacks, men or women, discrimination is rarely benevolent and always divisive. No more clear and direct constitutional limitation on the power of state and local governments exists than the command of equal protection of the laws. Yet, this promise remains routinely violated, more than a century and a quarter after the abolition of slavery and 39 years after *Brown* v. *Board of Education*. Typically, the victims are ordinary citizens who are innocent of any wrongdoing—people such as Rosa Parks, Stuart Marsh, Demond Crawford, or Stanley Dea.

As long as government retains the power to discriminate in favor of or against individuals on the basis of irrational factors such as race, demagogues and misguided social engineers will arise to invoke that power. Fortunately, the Constitution provides recourse to individuals who are victimized by invidious government discrimination. Perhaps one day soon, perhaps after enough shameful episodes of grassroots tyranny, the guarantee of equality under law will finally be fully vindicated.

PART III

THE FUTURE

11. Liberty, Community, and the Future of Federalism

> The function of Liberalism in the past was that of putting a limit to the powers of kings. The function of true Liberalism in the future will be that of putting a limit to the powers of Parliaments.
>
> —Herbert Spencer[1]

The preceding chapters demonstrate that none of us, no matter how innocent or how sophisticated, is immune from grassroots tyranny. The scope and power of local government today extends to virtually all facets of the everyday lives of ordinary people. All too often, that power is exercised by officials whose names we don't know, in ways that are antithetical to most of the basic principles of a free society.

Considering the emphasis the Framers of the Constitution placed on protecting individual sovereignty against oppressive actions by both national and state governments, it is remarkable how vulnerable we now are to abuses of power by governments at every level. Yet, although citizens and political pundits alike often pay a great deal of attention to national politics and to the need to constrain the power of national government, few of us pay much attention to the even greater threat from governments in our own backyards.

This situation has not arisen overnight. The evolution toward an ever-growing government leviathan at the local level has been fueled over the course of many decades by several influences. The legislative and executive branches at the national and state levels have grown far larger than ever expected. New forms of government such as regulatory agencies, regional authorities, and planning boards have taken on breathtaking new powers, yet are largely

---

[1]Herbert Spencer, *The Man versus the State*, in *Selected Works of Herbert Spencer* (New York: D. Appleton & Co., 1892), p. 411.

hidden from view and immune to democratic processes. As the Framers predicted, special-interest groups (once called "factions") have greedily manipulated government to their own ends. And the courts, which were designed by the Framers to act as the ultimate guardians of liberty, have to a large extent abdicated that role and instead have aided and abetted the other branches of government in their accretion of power at the expense of liberty.

How can we arrest the modern propensity toward grassroots tyranny? In particular, how can we do so without destroying the legitimate role of state and local governments, not the least of which consists of preventing an accumulation of power by the national government? And how can we do so without impeding the ability of communities to legitimately order and control their own affairs?

The solution is to return to the basic principles of a free society that are embedded in our constitutional form of government. Specifically, that requires a rediscovery and reinvigoration of the principles of federalism.

A New Framework for Federalism

The constitutional system of federalism is a roadmap, established throughout the Constitution but given substance mainly by the Ninth, Tenth, and Fourteenth Amendments. Federalism safeguards liberty in two essential ways: (1) by creating a balance of powers between national and state governments, thereby restraining the power of both; and (2) by establishing a hierarchy of constitutional values, at the top of which is individual liberty.

"The Framers' basic solution to the might of government," observes Bernard Siegan, "was to disperse and diffuse it."[2] The balance and separation of powers among the three branches of the national government was one method. Federalism was another. The Framers believed the two most powerful and reliable guardians of liberties would be the federal judiciary and the state governments.[3] But they also feared state governments, which they sought to check by creating constitutional limits on state power and by

[2]Bernard H. Siegan, "Majorities May Limit the People's Liberties Only When Authorized to Do So by the Constitution," *San Diego Law Review* 27 (1990): 309, 356.

[3]James Madison, "Speech to the House Explaining His Proposed Amendment and His Notes for the Amendment Speech," in *The Rights Retained by the People*, ed. Randy E. Barnett, (Fairfax, Va.: George Mason University Press, 1989), pp. 60–61.

vesting authority in the national government to curb abuses of that power. James Madison hoped that with this dispersion of powers under the Constitution, national and state governments would "resist and frustrate the measures of each other."[4]

As Justice Lewis Powell remarked in his dissenting opinion in *Garcia* v. *San Antonio Metropolitan Transit Authority,* "The constitutionally mandated balance of power between the States and the Federal Government" is "a balance designed to protect our fundamental liberties."[5] To preserve this balance requires a rigorous respect for federalism, but also a rejection of any concept of federalism that views state autonomy as an end in itself. The Tenth Amendment establishes a general constitutional presumption in favor of decentralized government—the government that is closest to the people. However, it does so not because it glorifies such governments as ends in themselves, but because it presumes such governments generally will promote individual liberty.

The Framers of the Constitution were clear in their definition of "liberty": the basic right of all individuals to control their own lives free from arbitrary or excessive government interference. According to William Blackstone's definition, which was embraced by the Framers,

> [Civil liberty] is no other than natural liberty so far restrained by human laws (and no farther) as is necessary and expedient for the general advantage of the publick. Hence we may collect that the law, which restrains a man from doing mischief to his fellow citizens, though it diminishes the natural, increases the civil liberty of mankind: but every wanton and causeless restraint of the will of the subject, whether practiced by a monarch, a nobility, or a popular assembly, is a degree of tyranny. Nay, that even laws themselves, whether made with or without our consent, if they regulate and constrain our conduct, are laws destructive of liberty. . . . [T]hat constitution or frame of government, that system of laws, is alone calculated to maintain civil liberty, which leaves the subject entire master of his own conduct,

[4]Harold M. Hyman, "Federalism: Legal Fiction and Historical Artifact?" *Brigham Young University Law Review* 15 (1987): 905, 918.

[5]*Garcia* v. *San Antonio Metropolitan Transit Authority,* 469 U.S. 528, 572 (1985) (Powell, J., dissenting).

> except in those points wherein the public good requires
> some direction or restraint.[6]

That the highest value in the constitutional system of federalism is not states' rights but individual liberty is clearly established by the Ninth Amendment—the amendment that, as Siegan writes, "[p]erhaps more than any other . . . discloses the intended constitutional relationship between governor and governed."[7] Justice Arthur Goldberg explained this relationship in his concurring opinion in *Griswold* v. *State of Connecticut*:

> While the Ninth Amendment—and indeed the entire Bill
> of Rights—originally concerned restrictions on *federal*
> power, the subsequently enacted Fourteenth Amendment
> prohibits the States from abridging fundamental personal
> liberties. And, the Ninth Amendment, in indicating that
> not all such liberties are specifically mentioned in the first
> eight amendments, is surely relevant in showing the exis-
> tence of other personal rights, now protected from state, as
> well as federal, infringement.[8]

Randy Barnett argues that "the Ninth Amendment can be viewed as establishing a general constitutional presumption in favor of individual liberty."[9] He explains,

> As a practical matter, we must choose between two funda-
> mentally different constructions of the Constitution. . . .
> Either we accept the presumption that in pursuing happi-
> ness persons may do whatever is not justly prohibited or
> we are left with a presumption that the government may
> do whatever is not expressly prohibited. The presence of
> the Ninth Amendment in the Constitution strongly sup-
> ports the first of these two presumptions.[10]

Although consistent with the original intent of the Constitution, a presumption in favor of liberty would mark a major change in

---

[6]William Blackstone, *Commentaries*, quoted in Siegan, pp. 351–52.

[7]Ibid., p. 325.

[8]*Griswold* v. *Connecticut*, 381 U.S. 479, 493 (1965) (Goldberg, J., concurring) (emphasis in original).

[9]Barnett, p. 41.

[10]Ibid., p. 43.

contemporary jurisprudence, which presumes government power is properly exercised unless it infringes upon one of a limited number of rights explicitly protected by the Constitution (such as due process, equal protection against racial discrimination, and freedom of speech). Instead, a presumption in favor of liberty would mean that any time the government interferes with individual autonomy, it must justify its action as a proper exercise of an explicitly delegated power or as necessary to promote public health, safety, or welfare. As Siegan explains, such a presumption in favor of liberty would operate in the following manner:

> In suits challenging the validity of restraints [upon human freedom], the government would have the burden of persuading a court . . . first, that the legislation serves important governmental objectives; second, that the restraint imposed by government is substantially related to the achievement of these objectives, that is . . . the fit between the means and ends must be close; and third, that a similar result cannot be achieved by less drastic means [11]

The instant objection that arises to such a proposal is that it will foster judicial activism. To the contrary, a judiciary that consistently applies a presumption in favor of liberty will finally be fulfilling precisely the role assigned to the courts by the Constitution. Only the judiciary, whose members are appointed to lifetime terms and are relatively immune to political pressures, can effectively safeguard the precious freedoms that the Constitution was designed to protect. The courts were intended to defer to other branches of government with respect to the exercise of powers delegated to those branches by the Constitution, but the courts were also assigned the duty of protecting against abuses of liberty.[12] A judiciary that stands idly by while the other branches of government trample individual rights is a judiciary that has abdicated its most essential responsibility.

This abdication began in 1872 with the *Slaughter-House Cases*, in which the Court ruled that basic individual rights such as economic

[11]Siegan, p. 352.

[12]See Clint Bolick, *Changing Course: Civil Rights at the Crossroads* (New Brunswick, N.J.: Transaction Books, 1988), pp. 122–41. The model for the judiciary described here was first and most eloquently presented by Alexander Hamilton in *The Federalist* no. 78, in *The Federalist Papers* (New York: Modern Library, 1937).

liberty were not protected as privileges or immunities of citizenship under the Fourteenth Amendment. When the Court has an opportunity to do so, it should correct this grievous misreading of constitutional text and history by overturning *Slaughter-House*.

A constitutional presumption in favor of liberty also would curb judicial activism of the type that establishes different degrees of protection depending on the liberty involved, and which derives affirmative rights from government entitlements while at the same time reading fundamental liberties out of the Constitution. The judiciary of the 1960s created welfare rights and all manner of procedural protections for criminal defendants while simultaneously abandoning protection of economic liberty, freedom of contract, and private-property rights. The judiciary of the 1990s has modestly increased protection for property rights while eroding protection for freedom of speech and free exercise of religion. The Constitution does not create such a dichotomy among rights. It recognizes that individuals retain primary control over their own destinies, gives government the power to regulate and safeguard that liberty, and creates mechanisms to restrain abuses of liberty.

As I have argued throughout this book, federalism is one of those mechanisms. A comprehensive understanding of the principles of federalism requires rejection of the ideological extremes that currently dominate debates about federalism. State governments are neither constitutionally irrelevant, as some would argue, nor are they constitutionally glorified as if they were ends in themselves. Adherence to the core values of federalism means a preference for decentralized government, *primarily* as a means of protecting individual liberty.

The principles of federalism do not dictate a particular outcome in any given conflict between national and state governments or between government and individuals. But they do establish a fairly clear hierarchy of values. The following guidelines provide a framework for applying the principles of federalism:

1. In disputes between the national government and state or local governments that do not raise issues of individual liberty, the principles of federalism establish a preference in favor of the government that is closest to the people, unless the national government is properly exercising an explicitly delegated constitutional power.

182

2. In disputes between the national government and state or local governments that do raise issues of individual liberty, the principles of federalism establish a preference in favor of liberty, unless the governmental entity restricting liberty is properly exercising an explicitly delegated constitutional power.

3. In disputes between individuals and government at any level raising issues of individual liberty, the principles of federalism establish a presumption in favor of liberty, which the government may overcome only by demonstrating that it is exercising its delegated powers in a reasonable manner.

This framework reflects the essential meaning of federalism, in which great value is assigned to decentralized government, and paramount value to individual liberty. By applying these principles of federalism to legal issues that involve clashes among the national government, the states, and individuals, we can finally restore a vital pillar of republican government that is essential to a free society.

Federalism in the Real World

Applying these principles in the real world is a difficult task. In the first instance, members of the executive and legislative branches must observe the boundaries of their legitimate power. This requires enormous self-restraint to resist the temptation to expand government power at the expense of individual liberty, and sometimes means denying majoritarian sentiments. Fortunately, evidence exists that some local governments are returning some power to individuals, as reflected by the growing trend toward privatization of services now provided by local governments.[13]

When executive and legislative officials fail to exercise appropriate restraint, the task of applying the principles of federalism falls to the judiciary. Here too, restraint and fidelity to constitutional principles is necessary. The judiciary must be diligent in defending individual rights (for no other branch is capable ultimately of vindicating them), but it must defer to democratic processes in matters that fall within the scope of legitimate government power. But

---

[13]See, for example, Jay Mathews, "Push to Privatize Public Works Reported," *Washington Post*, April 20, 1991, p. A11.

the courts have proven remarkably inconsistent in observing these boundaries, in large part because few of them have applied a coherent vision of federalism.

How would the principles of federalism operate in specific instances? It is useful to consider some examples.

The Supreme Court's 1985 decision in *Garcia* provides a good starting point. In *Garcia*, the city transit authority sought an exemption from the national Fair Labor Standards Act. The Court's majority held that the imposition of the act by the national government was an appropriate exercise of the commerce power, and that the state must look to the political process for the relief it sought. The four dissenters argued that the displacement of state authority over its labor contracts in the name of the federal contract power was destructive of federalism and individual liberty.

In applying the principles of federalism to the facts of *Garcia*, the dissenters were correct. This case presents a clash between local and national power, so the Court should begin with a presumption in favor of decentralized authority. Although the majority invoked the commerce power to justify the national regulation, that power is not sufficiently explicit to override the Tenth Amendment's presumption in favor of decentralized authority. Moreover, the transit authority's action in this case promoted individual liberty, in that it sought to preserve the autonomy of the employer and employees to freely bargain over the terms and conditions of employment without federal regulatory interference. Viewing *Garcia* either as a national versus local government dispute or as a dispute involving fundamental individual liberties, the case was incorrectly decided.

A different result should occur if, for example, a state imposes a more stringent regulation on economic activities than does the national government. For instance, Robert Bork (surprisingly) argues that extensive state food and drug labeling regulations are "preempted" by less onerous national regulations. Bork urges that "the fact that the pendulum has swung too far in the direction of centralization should not produce a knee-jerk hostility to federal power."[14] In this instance, the national power is exercised legitimately under the commerce clause, which was designed to limit

---

[14]Robert H. Bork, *Federalism and Federal Regulation: The Case of Product Labeling* (Washington: Washington Legal Foundation, 1991), p. 4.

parochial economic regulations by state governments. Moreover, the national power is exercised in a fashion consistent with individual liberty, which is the highest value of federalism. In a case like this, a court should strike down the state regulation.

To cite one further example of economic regulation, both the national and state governments have laws requiring private firms that contract with the government to pay prevailing union wages to their workers. These protectionist laws limit the ability of employers and employees to freely bargain over wages, with devastating consequences for workers outside the economic mainstream.[15] In a legal challenge to such laws at either the state or national level, the Court should begin with a presumption in favor of liberty and require the government to demonstrate that the laws are necessary to achieve a legitimate government objective. If the government is unable to justify the regulations, the laws should be struck down.

The principles of federalism do not apply only to instances wherein government is attempting to restrict liberty. Both national and state governments are free to take steps to protect individual rights against each other. The federal government, for example, should extend federal antitrust laws to explicitly proscribe anticompetitive regulations by local governments. Because the power to regulate interstate commerce was given to the national government precisely to protect free markets and guard against parochial state economic regulations, expansion of antitrust laws in this manner would not violate federalism principles. Similarly, as I have advocated elsewhere,[16] the national government could pass economic liberty legislation pursuant to its enforcement powers under the Fourteenth Amendment that would protect entrepreneurs against regulatory barriers that are not necessary to satisfy important public health or safety concerns.

In the same manner, states can (and sometimes do) establish protections for liberties such as freedom of speech or private-property rights that go beyond federal constitutional guarantees. Such

[15]Indeed, the federal Davis-Bacon Act, passed in 1931, was explicitly motivated in part by the desire to limit competition for jobs from black workers. See Bolick, *Changing Course*, pp. 101–2; and David Bernstein, "The Davis-Bacon Act: Let's Bring Jim Crow to an End," Cato Institute Briefing Paper no. 17 (January 18, 1993).

[16]See Clint Bolick, "Removing Barriers to Entrepreneurial Opportunities," in *Breaking the Chain: Empowerment Policy for the 1990s* (Washington: American Legislative Exchange Council), p. 60.

efforts are consistent with a concept of federalism in which a balance of powers exists between national and state governments, to the benefit of individual liberty.

These examples illustrate the proper balance among national government, local governments, and individual liberty. They recognize an extensive realm for the permissible exercise of government power while providing a check against unjustified deprivations of individual liberty. The framework of federalism, formed from the confluence of the Ninth, Tenth, and Fourteenth Amendments, does not deprive government of all or even most of its current regulatory power. Rather, it merely places the burden on government to demonstrate that its regulation of individuals is a reasonable exercise of a delegated power.

In sum, application of the principles of federalism, as Calvin R. Massey maintains, would "provide more life to the states as protectors of the liberties of their citizens against federal encroachment," while at the same time operating "to prevent the federal or state governments from invading the reserved personal liberties of the people."[17] In so doing, the federalism would no longer be an empty constitutional vessel or a subterfuge for grassroots tyranny. It would be a bulwark of a free society, finally fulfilling the aspirations of the Framers.

Federalism and Community

Will efforts to curb grassroots tyranny work against equally vital efforts to restore a sense of community in America?

The answer is no, and indeed to the contrary. Returning to a theme sounded earlier, communities and local governments are not the same. A community is a voluntary association of people; a local government is a political entity that may or may not coincide with a community. The principles of federalism outlined here only curtail the capacity to use the coercive power of government to violate individual rights. They do not at all limit the ability of voluntary communities to set rules for their members.[18]

---

[17]Calvin R. Massey, "Federalism and Fundamental Rights: The Ninth Amendment," in Barnett, p. 336.

[18]These boundaries between voluntary community rules and the use of coercive government power in a manner adverse to individual liberty are often confused. See, for example, "The Flag and the Community," *Wall Street Journal*, June 18, 1990, arguing in favor of a community's "right" to outlaw flag burning.

Indeed, these federalism principles strengthen communities in two important ways. First, federalism's preference for decentralized power would give local governments greater power relative to governments at any other level. Second, the growth of government at every level is antithetical to the concept of community, for it coercively substitutes political rules for the consensual shared values that are the essence of community. The existence of communities depends upon the freedom of association of their members, a liberty whose protection has been diminished greatly in recent years in the face of regulations imposed by every level of government. As communities adopt rules or values that are contrary to government regulation, a constitutional presumption in favor of liberty would force government to justify such restrictions, thereby protecting communities against government.

Again, the trend toward decentralization will enhance community power. Services previously provided by governments, such as urban transportation, law enforcement, and low-income housing, are being turned over to neighborhood groups as part of the effort to "empower" communities.[19] In Wisconsin, the state supreme court recently upheld the Milwaukee Parental Choice Program, which allows low-income youngsters to opt out of failing public schools and instead use their state education funds in private community schools.[20] School choice and other reforms that transfer power from government to the people are responsive to the pluralism of our society and enhance the ability of individuals to form community institutions that have eroded in the face of expanding government.

Decentralization of power and individual rights—the cornerstones of federalism—are also the life blood of communities. The renaissance of these principles may mark as well the rekindling of community.

Federalism and Freedom

The survival of a free society rests upon the recognition that the sanctity of one person's freedom depends upon the protection of

[19]Sam Staley, "Bigger Is Not Better: The Virtues of Decentralized Local Government," Cato Institute Policy Analysis no. 166 (January 21, 1992), pp. 24–32.

[20]*Davis* v. *Grover*, 480 N.W.2d 460 (Wis. 1992). The author had the privilege of defending the program in court on behalf of low-income parents.

everyone else's freedom. As the Fifth Circuit Court of Appeals has observed,

> It is not the courts alone who are bound to safeguard these freedoms. Executives and legislatures, from the nation's capital to the smallest village, and most of all the people themselves, are called upon by our Constitution to respect, enforce and cherish these principles of liberty and personal autonomy.[21]

The principles of federalism are not self-executing. Ultimately, the future of federalism—and of our basic freedoms—depends not so much on governments or courts as on how much Americans themselves cherish their freedoms. If we value exercising dominion over others more than we value liberty, we quickly will discover that our own liberty is compromised as government power grows and the realm of personal autonomy shrinks. Likewise, if people are complacent about their freedoms, little incentive will exist for governments to resist the temptation to expand power or for courts to curb abuses of power.

Individuals can do a great deal to protect against grassroots tyranny. Education is essential: citizen watchdog groups can be especially effective in monitoring government agencies, particularly those whose activities largely are outside the public eye, to expose abuses of individual rights. Policy activists should press for greater protections of individual rights at both the state and national levels. Individuals, depending on their philosophical disposition, can support groups such as the Institute for Justice, the Cato Institute, the National Taxpayers Union, Citizens for a Sound Economy, the American Civil Liberties Union, and others that fight various forms of grassroots tyranny.

These matters are far from academic. Myriad contemporary issues revolve around questions of federalism and the relationship between individuals and their government. But many people who argue about these issues ignore or distort the principles of federalism in the quest to achieve a particular outcome. The phenomenon of situational federalism, wherein the principles change depending

[21] *Aladdin's Castle, Inc.* v. *City of Mesquite*, 630 F.2d 1029, 1046 (5th Cir. 1980), *rev'd in part and remanded*, 455 U.S. 283 (1982), *opinion extended*, 713 F.2d 137 (5th Cir. 1983).

upon the desired outcome, destroys federalism's vitality as a pillar of our freedoms and self-government.

More than two centuries ago, confronting tyranny in his own time, Thomas Paine wrote that "we must return to first principles . . . and *think*, as if we were the first men that thought."[22] My goals in writing this book were two: to clearly identify the first principles of federalism that are essential to a free society, and to describe the regime of grassroots tyranny that has resulted from the abandonment of those principles. By presenting a model by which to implement the principles of federalism, I hope to help reinvigorate that venerable doctrine to meet the many challenges to liberty in our nation's third century.

Local government is an essential and enduring part of our democratic system. So is freedom. The two need not conflict. But as local government has grown into a leviathan, the threat to our freedoms is increasingly close to home. A rediscovery of the first principles of federalism will help Americans to protect their most sacred birthright: the power to control their own destinies.

[22]Quoted in Harry Hayden Clark, ed., *Thomas Paine and the Rights of Man* (New York: Charles Scribner's Sons, 1971), p. xiv (emphasis in original).

Index

Hyman, Harold M., 58, 68, 179

Ihil, Gwen, 100, 101
Individual liberty
 federalism, as protector of,
  overview, 13–18
 as purpose of federalism, 7
 states as guardians of, 38
Innerst, Carol, 137
Isikoff, Michael, 105

Jacobson, Carolyn, 128
Jefferson, David J., 104
Jefferson, Thomas, oppression by
 government, letter from Madison, 39
Johnson, Andrew, 61
Johnson v. *Transportation Agency*, 480
 U.S. 616 (1987), 88

Kammen, Michael, 26
Keen, Judy, 123
Korematsu v. *United States*, 323 U.S. 214
 (1944), 167
Kurland, Philip B., 68

Larry P. v. *Riles*, 495 F. Supp. 926
 (1979), 163
Levy, Leonard W., 148, 149
Liberty, 13–18
Licensing laws, 141–46
Lilie, Stuart A., 16
Lincoln, Abraham, civil liberty
 violation, 58–59
Linden, New Jersey, 1–3
Lloyd Corp. v. *Tanner*, 407 U.S. 551
 (1972), 90
Local government
 and community, distinction, 95–96
 hidden power of, 97–109
 regulation of individual rights,
  overview, 1–9
Lochhead, Carolyn, 115
Lochner v. *New York*, 198 U.S. 45
 (1905), 25, 73
Lofgren, Charles A., 69
Logan, David A., 38, 47, 54, 56–57, 59,
 60, 62
Lucas v. *South Carolina Coastal Council*,
 112 S.Ct. 2886 (1992), 113–14

Macedo, Stephen, 17, 18, 21, 45
Maddox, William S., 16
Madison, James, 14, 15, 18, 37–40, 43,
 44, 46, 178

Majoritarian process, 22
Maltz, Earl M., 28
Mapplethorpe, Robert, exhibition,
 123–26
Marcus, Ruth, 104, 105
Massey, Calvin, 186
Masters, Kim, 123
Mathews, Jay, 183
McDowell, Gary L., 54
Meese, Edwin, III, 25, 26, 87
Merline, John, 138, 139
Metropolitan Life Insurance Co. v. *Ward*,
 470 U.S. 869 (1985), 25
Miller v. *California*, 413 U.S. 15 (1973),
 127
Monnell v. *Department of Social Services*,
 436 U.S. 658 (1978), 108
Monopoly, taxicab, 146–47
Moore v. *City of East Cleveland*, 431 U.S.
 494 (1977), 160
Morley, Felix, 13, 23, 40, 45, 46–47, 50,
 53

Narrett, David E., 41
National League of Cities v. *Usery*, 426
 U.S. 833 (1976), 31–33, 35–36
Near v. *Minnesota*, 283 U.S. 697 (1931),
 27
New Deal, 16, 26
New Orleans v. *Dukes*, 427 U.S. 297
 (1976), 118
New State Ice Co. v. *Liebmann*, 285 U.S.
 262 (1932), 27
New York City, 115–17
Ninth Amendment, 49–52
 decentralized power, promulgation
  of, 14
 federalism doctrine in, 20
 wording of, 49
Nollan v. *California Coastal Commission*,
 483 U.S. 825 (1987), 73, 118
Nozario, Sonia L., 104

Obscenity, 127
Ordaz, John, 128
Original intent, doctrine of, 18–19

Paine, Thomas, 109
Participatory democracy, 7
Patterson, Bennett B., 50
People, sovereignty in, 21–22
Pierce v. *Society of Sisters*, 268 U.S. 510
 (1925), 73, 156
Plessy v. *Ferguson*, 163 U.S. 537 (1896),
 72–73, 166

Cato Institute

Founded in 1977, the Cato Institute is a public policy research foundation dedicated to broadening the parameters of policy debate to allow consideration of more options that are consistent with the traditional American principles of limited government, individual liberty, and peace. To that end, the Institute strives to achieve greater involvement of the intelligent, concerned lay public in questions of policy and the proper role of government.

The Institute is named for *Cato's Letters,* libertarian pamphlets that were widely read in the American Colonies in the early 18th century and played a major role in laying the philosophical foundation for the American Revolution.

Despite the achievement of the nation's Founders, today virtually no aspect of life is free from government encroachment. A pervasive intolerance for individual rights is shown by government's arbitrary intrusions into private economic transactions and its disregard for civil liberties.

To counter that trend, the Cato Institute undertakes an extensive publications program that addresses the complete spectrum of policy issues. Books, monographs, and shorter studies are commissioned to examine the federal budget, Social Security, regulation, military spending, international trade, and myriad other issues. Major policy conferences are held throughout the year, from which papers are published thrice yearly in the *Cato Journal.* The Institute also publishes the quarterly magazine *Regulation.*

In order to maintain its independence, the Cato Institute accepts no government funding. Contributions are received from foundations, corporations, and individuals, and other revenue is generated from the sale of publications. The Institute is a nonprofit, tax-exempt, educational foundation under Section 501(c)3 of the Internal Revenue Code.

CATO INSTITUTE
1000 Massachusetts Ave., N.W.
Washington, D.C. 20001

About the Author

Clint Bolick is vice president and litigation director at the Institute for Justice, a Washington-based public interest law firm. He is the author of two previous books, *Changing Course: Civil Rights at the Crossroads* and *Unfinished Business: A Civil Rights Strategy for America's Third Century*. He has sued city governments from Washington to Chicago to Los Angeles on behalf of civil rights, economic liberty, and free speech.